Prisoner of Pinochet

Critical Human Rights

Series Editors
Steve J. Stern ❦ Scott Straus

Books in the series Critical Human Rights emphasize research that opens new ways to think about and understand human rights. The series values in particular empirically grounded and intellectually open research that eschews simplified accounts of human rights events and processes.

After bombing the presidential palace in downtown Santiago on September 11, 1973, and taking control of Chile, what would the military junta led by General Augusto Pinochet do with high officials of the vanquished democratic government of Salvador Allende? The dictatorship saw adversaries as war enemies rather than as citizens. The junta intended not an interim coup to restore order but a radical makeover of politics and society, backed by force. This scheme left no room for dissident political leaders. Allende committed suicide before soldiers stormed the presidential palace. Some high officials eluded capture and escaped into exile, while others were assassinated, whether in Chile or abroad. Many ended up political prisoners. Banished to Dawson Island near Chilean Antarctica, former cabinet officials such as Sergio Bitar, Allende's minister of mining, endured a regime of brutal weather, poor diet, and forced labor. In a memoir whose matter-of-fact tone enhances its poignancy and insight, Bitar tells a human rights story both unique and universal. It is the unique story of Pinochet's Chile, a dictatorship that destroyed a once vibrant democracy and galvanized international human rights concerns. It is the universal story of political prisoners whose world has collapsed, yet who somehow defend their human decency and dignity—and, therefore, the possibility of hope.

Prisoner of Pinochet

*My Year
in a Chilean Concentration Camp*

Sergio Bitar

Translated by
Erin Goodman

Foreword and notes by
Peter Winn

The University of Wisconsin Press

The University of Wisconsin Press
1930 Monroe Street, 3rd Floor
Madison, Wisconsin 53711-2059
uwpress.wisc.edu

3 Henrietta Street, Covent Garden
London WCE 8LU, United Kingdom
eurospanbookstore.com

Printed in the United States of America

This book may be available in a digital edition.

Library of Congress Cataloging-in-Publication Data

Names: Bitar, Sergio, author. | Goodman, Erin E., translator. | Winn, Peter, writer of foreword.
Title: Prisoner of Pinochet: my year in a Chilean concentration camp / Sergio Bitar; translated by Erin Goodman; foreword and notes by Peter Winn.
Other titles: *Isla 10*. English | Critical human rights.
Description: Madison, Wisconsin: The University of Wisconsin Press, [2017] | Series: Critical human rights | Originally published as *Isla 10*, by Sergio Bitar, ©1987 by Sergio Bitar and Pehuen Editores. | Includes bibliographical references and index.
Identifiers: LCCN 2017010438 | ISBN 9780299313708 (cloth: alk. paper)
Subjects: LCSH: Bitar, Sergio. | Political prisoners—Chile—Biography. | Chile—Politics and government—1973-
Classification: LCC F3101.B58 A3 2017 | DDC 983.06/5092 [B]—dc23
LC record available at https://lccn.loc.gov/2017010438

Contents

Illustrations

following page 62

Foreword

In my lifetime I have experienced two traumatic 9/11's. As a New Yorker, I lived through September 11, 2001, with its aerial attack on the Twin Towers, and its indelible memory resonates with me.

But I also lived through and cannot forget my memories of another violent 9/11: September 11, 1973, in Chile, the date of the bloody military coup that overthrew the democratically elected government of President Salvador Allende. That 9/11 also culminated in an aerial attack that left a symbolic building in flames, but that aerial attack was by the Chilean Air Force and the building its planes destroyed was Chile's presidential palace, with the country's president inside. The dead that day included President Allende, and the violent coup that ousted him destroyed Chile's democracy for almost two decades.

After a distinguished career as a congressional deputy, cabinet minister, and senator, Allende was elected president in 1970 as the candidate of a broad leftist coalition, on a platform of pioneering a nonviolent, democratic road to a Democratic Socialism that included an agrarian reform, as well as the nationalization of mines, banks, and large industries, with worker participation in their management. By 1973, Allende's government had made major advances along this Democratic Socialist road. The goal of the coup was to reverse those advances and block that road.

The military coup led to the seventeen-year dictatorship of General Augusto Pinochet, a dictatorship that massively violated human rights and was responsible for the deaths of more than three thousand Chileans—a toll similar to the number of deaths on September 11, 2001. It also imprisoned and tortured more than 38,000 Chileans in more than 1,100 clandestine centers, concentration camps, and military barracks.

When the attack began on La Moneda, Chile's presidential palace, I was across the square. I was fortunate to survive the battle that claimed the lives of more than one bystander. Like September 11, 2001, in New York, the events and experience of September 11, 1973, are indelible in my memory and have reshaped my life since then, making me a human rights activist and a historian of Chile, who has published books on the causes and consequences of the coup in both the United States and Chile, in English and in Spanish. For me, as for millions of Chileans, the coup of September 11, 1973, marked a great divide, a before and after that did not disappear from our memories when the Pinochet dictatorship came to an end in 1990.

In the wake of the 1973 coup, I was detained and interrogated in the military barracks where many of those who were with Allende in La Moneda were tortured and executed for the "crime" of defending the democratically elected government. I was more fortunate. I was neither tortured nor executed, only expelled from the country. In Boston I would write my account of the history that led to that coup alongside Sergio Bitar, a political exile from Chile at Harvard who was writing *his* analysis of where Allende's Road to Socialism was right and where it went wrong.

Bitar was a Harvard-educated economist when he joined the Christian Left in 1971, a new party of talented leaders, most of whom were disillusioned ex–Christian Democrats. The Christian Left supported Allende's democratic Road to Socialism and in mid-1971 joined his Popular Unity coalition. Allende's first year as president was successful. Keynesian economic policies revived a recessed economy and promoted consumption by the poorest Chilean families whose incomes increased on average by 30 percent, a reflection of a dramatic shift of nearly 10 percent of the national income from business owners to wage earners. That year also witnessed major advances toward a Democratic Socialism, and a leftist majority in national municipal elections was viewed as a mandate for Allende's program.

Yet by the end of Allende's first year in office, there were signs of economic problems and shifts in political momentum. Bitar was one of the first inside Allende's government to warn that the economic policies that had been successful in reviving a recessed economy in 1970 were leading by the end of 1971 to accelerating inflation, growing budget deficits, consumer shortages, and other economic dislocations. By 1972 Bitar had become one of Allende's top economic advisers, and in 1973 he became minister of mines, a key position in a country dependent on copper exports for three-quarters of its hard currency income.

In October 1972 the Allende government survived an opposition-led economic stoppage intended to create conditions for a military coup. Then, in midterm congressional elections in March 1973, the Popular Unity coalition actually increased its seats in the congress, denying Allende's Rightist and Centrist opponents the two-thirds vote they needed to impeach him.

With no elections scheduled before the end of Allende's projected six-year term as president, the opposition had no legal way to oust him and reverse the "revolutionary process" that he led. So they began banging on the barracks doors, pressing the military to intervene, as did—behind the scenes—the US government, whose complicity in the coup and the dictatorship that followed has been revealed by declassified documents and a US Senate investigation. The Chilean Army had a constitutionalist tradition of nonintervention in that country's politics, which its commander in chief, General Carlos Prats, upheld, as had his predecessor, General Rene Schneider, who as a result was assassinated in 1970 by the extreme Right in a plot orchestrated by the CIA. But by August 1973, economic dislocations, social tensions, and political polarization had politicized the armed forces as well as civil society, and Prats was forced to resign. He recommended to Allende as his successor his second in command, General Augusto Pinochet, who Prats considered an apolitical soldier's soldier who would keep the army in line. Prats was mistaken. Less than three weeks later, Pinochet led the violent coup that ousted Allende and put an end to democracy and Allende's Socialist road, as well as the rule of law and the army's tradition of nonintervention in Chile's politics.

Chileans had long expected a coup, and many favored a "soft coup" that would calm things down and then return power to elected civilian leaders. But few expected the coup to be so violent and to lead to a seventeen-year dictatorship that would make Chile notorious for human rights abuses and political repression. Most would vote against that dictatorship when they were given the chance in the 1988 plebiscite that Pinochet lost decisively, leading to the inauguration of an elected civilian president in 1990.

Sergio Bitar was fortunate that he survived the violent coup and its repressive aftermath. But he would have to survive a harsh imprisonment in an Antarctic concentration camp as well, along with other leaders of the Allende government and the Popular Unity coalition of political parties and social movements that supported its Chilean road to Socialism.

It is that story that Sergio Bitar tells so eloquently in *Isla 10* (his name and identity as a prisoner), the memoir that he wrote in the United States during his ten-year exile, after his release from confinement and before his return to Chile. There he became a leader of Chile's democratic transition, a founder and president of the Party for Democracy (PPD), as well as a senator and a minister in two governments.

This is both Bitar's own story and a collective memoir of the experience of the top leaders of the Allende government and the Popular Unity coalition. It is also a story of solidarity and resistance, of cruelty and humanity, one that compares to prison accounts from Stalin's Gulag. But most of all it is a story of the triumph of the human spirit despite all the attempts of a brutal dictatorship to break that spirit and destroy the humanity and solidarity of its prize prisoners.

Bitar tells his story with a terse understated style that makes it a page-turner, because you want to know what comes next and how it will all turn out. Significantly, the Spanish-language *Isla 10* has sold out thirteen editions in Chile and served as the base of an acclaimed cinema docudrama by one of Chile's leading filmmakers, with the role of Sergio Bitar played by one of Chile's leading actors. The book has also been published in translation in languages as diverse as Arabic and Italian, French and Albanian—and now in English as *Prisoner of Pinochet* in this faithful translation by Erin Goodman.

Like other thoughtful political prison memoirs, this is a book that transcends its national boundaries to illuminate a larger landscape. It should be required reading for all who care about democracy, human rights, and social justice.

PETER WINN

Tufts University
September 2016

Preface

   After I was freed and when I finished dictating this narrative, I felt a huge relief, like a weight lifting from my soul. I had just completed the most tragic period of my life. I had lived through an experience that I never could have imagined would happen in my country. I felt an urgency, a *necessity*, to convey this experience. Even if only one person read it, I felt it my duty to describe and alert him to what was going on in Chile.

   The events I relate took place between September 1973 and the end of 1974—the year I shared the harsh conditions of the Chilean concentration camps with several high-ranking officials from President Salvador Allende's constitutional government.

   When I was forced to leave my country at the end of 1974, I was emotional. I hadn't yet absorbed the importance of what had just happened. I didn't know what my future held: I aspired only to live again. I left Santiago on November 14, 1974, headed to Boston. The first stop was Washington, DC. Some friends were waiting for me there—Americans who had helped liberate me. The next day I met with Radomiro Tomic,[1] who was living there. He wanted to know how his daughter and son-in-law—Pedro Felipe Ramírez[2]—were doing, as Pedro Felipe had been detained with me. I started unloading my memories, sharing stories of our time in prison, and Tomic listened. After a couple of hours, he said, "Sergio, you should write down everything you're telling me, and do it now before you lose the intensity of what you've lived through."

   1. Radomiro Tomic was a Christian Democrat presidential candidate in 1970, as well as a party founder and leader of its left wing.
   2. Pedro Felipe Ramírez was a leader of the Christian Democratic left wing and then the Christian Left and had been minister of mining and of housing under Allende.

Next I went to New York. Orlando Letelier had been freed two months earlier and was waiting for me at the airport.[3] I still remember his face and the tears we shed when we hugged and realized we were together again, this time as free men, and still alive. I told him that I wanted to record what had happened on Dawson Island, and we exchanged ideas.

I spent 1975 at Harvard University. Each day when I returned home from work, I systematically dictated the story of my life in prison into a tape recorder. My wife, Kenny, painstakingly transcribed every tape. In this way it all was archived. More than ten years passed, but I felt at peace, because I knew that the pages that held my story were tucked away safely.

In 1984 I was allowed to return to Chile. After our exile ended, we had to get our lives together and bring with us to Chile only what was really important to us. I decided to go through the three hundred sheets of paper and type them up. In Caracas I asked Virginia Vidal for help doing this. As she transcribed, she would often ask me about some incident that wasn't clear, or some missing fact. That's when I realized something unexpected: as I reread the pages, my immediate memory was so blurry that I could only remember bits and pieces. At times it was as if someone else had written the words. It's interesting how the mind is capable of blocking difficult and potentially debilitating memories.

In 1986 we began the final revisions. Juan Andrés Piña took on the difficult task of polishing some of the dictated texts. We went over them, preserving the original spirit and the narrative style. If we made any larger revisions, it was in the interest of softening the passionate tone and some of the unavoidable emotionalism apparent in the original version. As time passes, passion begins to dissipate and the story is distilled to its essence, free from adjectives and embellishments. But despite this polishing, this book is faithful to the first version that I dictated in 1975, and that was published in 1987.

I thought a lot about whether to publish this book at that moment in time, when Chile was still ruled by Pinochet's dictatorship: it's hard to know where

3. Orlando Letelier had been Allende's ambassador to the United States and later his defense minister. A fellow Socialist and close collaborator with Allende, Letelier was imprisoned with Bitar on Dawson Island. After his release and exile to the United States, Letelier became one of the key leaders of the opposition to the dictatorship. He was assassinated in 1976 by a car bomb on Embassy Row in Washington on the orders of General Manuel Contreras, head of the DINA (National Intelligence Directorate), which a US military attaché described as a "Chilean Gestapo." In 1995 Contreras was tried in Chile and jailed for that crime, which he claimed Pinochet had ordered. He died in prison in 2015.

the line is between prudence and cowardice, between courage and irresponsibility. Above all, I believe that this is useful testimony and I feel the duty to publish it.

I've been motivated by love for my country and inspired to defend the dignity of every man and woman. It is impossible to support in silence the injustice and tragedy that we lived through. My generation was born and lived in democracy, and we believed it would last forever. But negative forces exist in all societies, those of egotism and destruction, capable of inhuman acts.

It is the duty of all Chileans to prevent the events that I recount here from being repeated and to assure freedom of all. I don't want my children to experience what we lived through. For that to be possible, we must shed light on history and strive for justice.

This testimony is also an expression of solidarity for the men with whom I shared my imprisonment at Dawson. It is also a modest contribution to the recognition of the thousands of Chilean men and women who suffered most direly in these years.

I owe my wife the greatest debt of gratitude. In addition to her support and constant motivation through this difficult period, her careful work and persistence also made the telling of this story possible.

This book is dedicated to her.

S. B.

Acknowledgments

I had always wished that English speakers could read this story about the Chilean September 11. That dramatic experience in 1973 demonstrated how the loss of freedom and political imprisonment under dictatorships have universal characteristics. Keeping memory alive helps to motivate action and protect human rights and democracy everywhere. The idea of an English-language edition came up in a conversation at a conference on Memory and Democracy at Harvard University in the fall of 2013. The director of the David Rockefeller Center for Latin American Studies, Dr. Merilee Grindle, and other participants reacted enthusiastically to the idea. Our story of imprisonment and forced labor on an isolated and cold island at the south of the Magellan Strait, together with ministers, senators, and university presidents, could help younger generations to remain aware of the past.

US politics are a part of Chilean history. In the Cold War era, the Nixon administration supported the Pinochet coup. Nevertheless, at the same time many Americans helped people like me and contributed to putting an end to that long dictatorship. This book demonstrates how US–Latin American relations are and will continue to be contradictory: between those in the United States who truly support democracy and those who try to impose their economic and military interests at the expense of the very same values they purport to share.

I express my gratitude to the many generous people who made this version possible. My thanks to Erin Goodman for her continuous effort to make this translation available. She has been essential at every stage of the process. My Spanish editor, Jorge Barros, no longer with us, deserves our recognition for his courage and rigor in publishing the original edition in 1987, when Chile was still under a dictatorship. I also thank his team, and Juan Manuel Galan in particular, for providing original and unique materials that are included in the book. Peter Winn reviewed the translation and wrote an illuminating foreword for the American reader. My friend, our country's famous writer Isabel Allende, wrote wonderful lines when we were promoting, at great risk, the original Spanish edition. Her words are vivid and valid today. My friend Miguel Littin produced a film based on this book in 2009. Miguel has been a courageous fighter for a democratic world through his creativity. Moreover, his movie expanded the reach of our message. I also appreciate the University of Wisconsin Press's enthusiastic interest and commitment to Latin American studies, democracy, and memory.

S. B.

In the mid-1990s I had the good fortune of being selected as a Rotary Exchange Student and I was sent to a small city in the central valley of Chile. Those twelve months would set me on a lifelong path studying and working in the field of Latin American studies. Three years ago when I met Sergio Bitar, I proposed that we work together on an English-language translation of his memoir, to bring his story to so many people for whom it had previously been silent. I will always be grateful for his confidence in my abilities to render his voice into English. Many thanks also to Peter Winn for his willingness to give historical and political context to Sergio's story, which makes this book more robust. I am also grateful for the guidance and encouragement from Merilee Grindle, Kathy Eckroad, Marysa Navarro, June Erlick, Ned Strong, and Anna Deeny from Harvard University, and Marjorie Agosín from Wellesley College.

E. G.

Complete List
of Unidad Popular Prisoners
at Dawson Island

Clodomiro Almeyda, minister of external affairs
Vladimir Arellano, budgetary director
Sergio Bitar, minister of mining and minister of housing
Jaime Concha, mayor of Santiago
Luis Corvalán, senator and secretary general of the Partido Comunista de
    Chile (Chilean Communist Party)
Edgardo Enríquez, minister of education
Fernando Flores, minister of economy
Patricio Guijón, La Moneda medical doctor
Alejandro Jiliberto, representative
Arturo Jirón, minister of health
Alfredo Joignant, director of Policía de Investigaciones (Chilean equivalent
    of the Federal Bureau of Investigation)
Carlos Jorquera, Salvador Allende's press secretary
Enrique Kirberg, president of the Universidad Técnica del Estado
Miguel Lawner, director of the Corporación del Mejoramiento Urbano
    (Corporation for Urban Improvement)
Carlos Lazo, vice president of the Banco del Estado
Orlando Letelier, minister of defense
Maximiliano Marholz, councilman for Valparaíso
Luis Matte, minister of housing
Carlos Matus, president of the Banco Central
Hugo Miranda, senator
Carlos Morales, representative

Miguel Muñoz, managing treasurer of the Banco Central

Héctor Olivares, representative

Julio Palestro, manager of Polla Chilena de Beneficencia, a national lottery company

Tito Palestro, mayor of San Miguel

Aníbal Palma, minister of education

Walter Pinto, manager of ENAMI, the Chilean National Mining Corporation

Osvaldo Puccio Sr., secretary to Salvador Allende

Osvaldo Puccio Jr., law student

Pedro Felipe Ramirez, minister of mining and minister of housing

Aniceto Rodríguez, senator

Camilo Salvo, representative

Erick Schnake, senator

Andrés Sepúlveda, representative

Adolfo Silva, La Moneda official photographer

Hernán Soto, undersecretary of mining

Julio Stuardo, mayor of Santiago

Anselmo Sule, senator and president of the Partido Radical (Radical Party)

Ariel Tachi, mayor of Viña del Mar

Jorge Tapia, minister of education and minister of justice

Benjamín Teplisky, executive secretary of the Unidad Popular (Popular Unity Party)

Jaime Tohá, minister of agriculture

José Tohá, minister of defense and of the interior, vice president of Chile

Luis Vega, advisor to the Ministry of the Interior

Daniel Vergara, undersecretary of the interior

Sergio Vuskovic, mayor of Valparaíso

Leopoldo Zuljevic, customs overseer

Prisoner of Pinochet

Escuela Militar

On September 11, 1973, at around eight o'clock in the morning, I received the telephone call from a party comrade. He anxiously told me there was a considerable movement of troops in downtown Santiago: they were blocking off the streets. From what he could tell, the movement confirmed the existence of a total coup d'état. In just a few seconds he verified what I had been suspecting for months.

It was so difficult to react in that moment. What was unfolding had seemed so unlikely to become reality: we had grown accustomed—like upholding a myth—to thinking that in Chile this sort of thing could never occur. We had the conviction that our country was immune to bloody coups like the one underway. We were certain that our democratic institutions were sufficiently flexible and that there would always be some public means through which we could transcend conflict. However, all this mythology that was ingrained in our lives, in our way of thinking, in our political analyses, fell apart. Once again we confirmed that if social tensions and the struggle to transform society reaches the point that it had in our country, it is impossible to insulate ourselves from the central problem of power, which at that moment was the military situation.

That's why I reacted so diffusely that morning: I wasn't sure *how* to act. I recalled what had happened on June 29, 1973, when something similar had occurred in the early morning hours. That attempted coup had been neutralized by the military itself.

On September 11 I had a meeting at the Corporación de Fomento (CORFO).[1] My first thought was to go downtown and to carry on with my

1. The Corporación de Fomento (CORFO) was the state development corporation created by the Popular Front government of 1938, which had the power to develop

day's activities, perhaps fueling my hope that one way or another this coup would also be dampened. However, when I turned on the radio I was able to appreciate the magnitude of what had happened: many stations were not transmitting, while others—I think the Magallanes radio station[2]—desperately informed the public that it was being bombed by planes, so that this would be its final transmission, its final attempt to communicate with some government authority. At the same time I started to hear the first euphoric cries coming from people in the street. My middle-class neighbors had started to gather joyously, celebrating the fall of the government. I intuited that on these occasions passion and a lack of control can take a turn for the dramatic, especially for the contested regime's partisans, and I became fearful for my children's safety. My first reaction was to get them out of the house and bring them elsewhere.

As we drove, the radio confirmed that the situation was getting desperate. The radio station's final transmission consisted of the last words of the president of the republic.[3] They were tragically beautiful words, revealing the definitive moment in which he knew that he was facing death. At that moment he reiterated his profound conviction in the necessity of social change in order to ensure the well-being of the people and reaffirmed his faith in the fundamental values of man: justice, freedom, and equality.

As members of his cabinet we had agreed that in an emergency of this nature, each of us would go to a designated place where we would be protected in case of any kind of prolonged conflict, until the situation had become clearer. So that morning I drove toward La Florida, where I waited in a room with people I trusted.[4] Fear had spread quickly. War airplanes concentrated

---

new industries. Under Allende, CORFO became the agency that nationalized industries and managed the public sector of the economy.

2. Radio Magallanes was one of several radio stations supportive of the Allende government, although most of the media was controlled by his opponents. On the day of the coup d'état, Radio Magallanes was the station that broadcast Allende's last words to his people.

3. President Salvador Allende's farewell speech to the nation, September 11, 1973: "Workers of my country, I have faith in Chile and its destiny. Other men will overcome this dark and bitter moment when treason seeks to prevail. Keep in mind that, much sooner than later, the great avenues will again be opened through which will pass free men to construct a better society. Long live Chile! Long live the people! Long live the workers!"

4. La Florida, today a suburb of Santiago and Chile's largest *comuna* (zone or neighborhood), was much less urbanized and poorer than it is today. The women who

their attention on the radio stations, attacking and bombing their antennae. Some radios continued to report using their emergency equipment. The community that I was in was located very close to a radio antenna. We could hear the bombings beginning in the morning. The airplanes passed very low to the ground with a deafening noise, sowing panic in men, women, and children. That day the curfew began very early. We could hear gunfire in the neighborhood throughout the day.

The news transmitted on the radio was dramatic. The situation was becoming more confusing by the minute, intensified by the silencing of almost all radio broadcasters. The stentorian new transmissions had begun on a radio station owned by the armed forces.

At around eleven o'clock in the morning, they announced that the president had a window of time to surrender. We didn't fully understand what surrendering would entail. The scenario conveyed by the radio stations—by now controlled by the military officers leading the uprising—was that there would be resistance at La Moneda, the presidential palace. This seemed impossible, and airborne attacks would be disproportionally violent.

They told the president that if he didn't leave La Moneda, it would be bombed. I couldn't help but remember the words that I had heard him say so many times, that he had reiterated just the day before at a lunch among ministers and former ministers: his objective was to avoid a civil war. He said it, he reiterated it, and he maintained it until the end: he did not want the blood of Chileans to flow. He also stated that he would stay in his post until the end. If the Unidad Popular (Popular Unity)[5] were defeated, he would go down with his government and its historic project. So I was convinced that if the bombings came to pass, the president would not come out alive. The attack occurred at noon. From where we were we could hear the strikes and runs of the bombers. This was not mentioned on the radio.

They asked people to stay in their homes, saying that the situation was under control. At about two or three o'clock in the afternoon, among other news (much of which consisted of calls for foreigners and certain political leaders to turn themselves in to the new authorities) and declarations of civilians supporting the military coup, the news of the death of the president was delivered

---

sheltered Bitar in their safe house had worked for his mother and known him since childhood. It was safe because it was unknown to political cadres and the personal loyalty of the women could be counted on.

5. Unidad Popular (Popular Unity) was Allende's political coalition, formed by an alliance of leftist parties.

briefly and succinctly. I remember the radio announcement verbatim: "At two o'clock in the afternoon, when the armed forces entered the presidential palace, they found there the lifeless body of Mr. Allende." Immediately afterward, with no commentary whatsoever, we could hear the voices of some business associates and political leaders of rightist parties signaling that our nation had been liberated and that once and for all the Chilean people would escape the totalitarian government of the Unidad Popular.

This is how the first events unfolded. Obviously the emotional impact provokes an incommensurable crisis. Many common people, like those around me, did not understand the ramifications of this news, did not really comprehend the full magnitude. For a while afterward, there were people who believed that the president was still alive and that he would come liberate them at some point in the future.

But it all ended there.

Meanwhile, on the radio they continued to read interminable lists of foreigners of all nationalities and of leftist politicians, calling on them to turn themselves in. Nobody had a notion of the extent of what was to come. As we learned later, many of the foreigners who answered the summons were disappeared or later found lifeless. Others barely escaped.

I was shaken by these events and didn't have a clear awareness of what everything meant. I tried to capture some news from Argentina or somewhere else on the shortwave radio to clarify what had happened. I held on to a hope that there would be something—some force, maybe even of divine origin— that could intervene and undo these occurrences. Tears welled permanently in my eyes. The sky darkened and machine-gun rounds sounded in the neighborhood, consisting of little houses made of thin metal or wood partitions, through which any bullet could cross, killing its occupants. People were terrified, hidden under their bed covers or on the floor.

We could still hear the radio stations announcing that there were certain areas of resistance in parts of Santiago and that the army was advancing toward them, especially to the factories on the industrial belts[6] and some university

---

6. The *cordón industrial* (industrial belt) was a territorial organization of manufacturing companies and their surrounding residential neighborhoods that enabled workers to circumvent the legal organization of Chilean labor by industry, so that factory workers in the same industrial belt could band together, even if they were, for example, a textile mill, a metallurgical plant, and a food production factory. The *cordones industriales* were largely Socialist in their leadership; the Communists who dominated the

campuses, such as the Universidad Técnica del Estado. They warned that the armed forces personnel would be relentless and that anyone who resisted would be executed on the spot. It wasn't until the next day that we heard that many Chileans had died.

Very early on September 12, I asked one of the people whose home I was staying in if they could call my house to see how my family was doing and if there was any news. My family told me that they had heard on a news program that morning at 7:00 a.m. that a new group of people was being summoned to appear at the Ministry of Defense. My name was among those called. At first I thought that it was some kind of mistake or confusion, but during the day I verified that it was true: the people summoned had until 6:00 p.m. of the next day to appear. Otherwise, they would be hunted down until they were found and arrested.

It was a tense night. I wasn't sure what to do, given such a dearth of information. The first reaction of anyone who feels that he has acted with honesty and transparency—even though he may have made some mistakes in the implementation of some policies—is to face the consequences, believing that the motivating principles of his life and of the lives of those around him are common values that all Chileans share. I vacillated a lot. I even remember dreaming that it might be a situation that lasted for months, rather than days, which one could deduce from the way that they were summoning us.

Very early the next day, I went out to find a pay phone despite the fact that the curfew hadn't been lifted, and I spoke directly with some friends and my family. My wife, Kenny—who had been contacted with an offer of asylum for me by some of the embassies—told me that it was my decision but that she thought it would be better to appear: if there was nothing to regret, there would be nothing to fear. Surely, she also suspected that if I didn't appear, and if the embassies were closed, then I would be hunted down, and if found, my life would be in danger. She also told me that on the radio, despite the fact that they were listing people alphabetically, my name had been announced at the end, as if they had added it at the last minute. Later, seeing it written in the newspapers, we discovered that this was because my last name had been misspelled with the letter V instead of B.

---

traditional labor union system within the Popular Unity coalition opposed them. The *cordones* played a major role in stalemating the October 1972 "bosses strike" and were hated and feared by the rightist opposition. Their factories and leaders were prime targets of military repression in the aftermath of the coup d'état.

I called several people and received very different opinions. Some had heard from military agents that there was nothing to fear and that most likely the group of Unidad Popular leaders that appeared would be rounded up and expelled from the country. According to others, the situation was less clear, because they hadn't been able to reach people at a higher level, people who hours before had been their friends and who would have been able to answer these questions.

There was a lot of confusion. Many of my colleagues who had been summoned said that they would appear. Others decided that it would be too risky. Without thinking about it too much and acting on spontaneous feelings and impulses, I decided to appear.

That morning, when the curfew was lifted, my wife came to bring me home and I spent some time with my children. My father was out of the country at that time. Some friends arrived, terrified, and they couldn't offer any opinion or advice; in difficult circumstances, most people are unprepared for the situation at hand, and few dare to bear the responsibility of orienting another.

And so, after a few hours at home, my wife and my mother took me to the Ministry of Defense, with enough clothing for a few days. Later I would learn that a few minutes after I had left my house, some friends had arrived to warn me not to present myself, because the scarce information they had gathered indicated that things were very violent and that I shouldn't trust anyone or anything. The declarations on the radio announcing that some former ministers had appeared and were in custody with no problems were false. One or two diplomats had also arrived at my parents' house, advising that the best thing to do would be to seek asylum.

So I went to the Ministry of Defense. We drove down the deserted main thoroughfare, the Alameda, surrounded by soldiers aiming in all directions and especially toward buildings, on the lookout for snipers. We approached downtown, the ministry. This was the headquarters of the coup.

I entered the ministry at 4:00 p.m. on September 13. Inside I met up with Jorge Tapia, former minister of education and justice, who had shown up as I had. I identified myself to a low-ranking officer who was at the entrance. After showing my ID card, I explained that I had been summoned on the radio. He brought me to different floors, where he asked others what he should do with a minister who had presented himself in response to the authorities. There was confusion. They brought me up to the fifth floor, to the sixth. Later I had to wait awhile. Finally someone named Lieutenant Zamorano of the general staff appeared. This officer, with sobriety and measured words, informed me that I would be transferred to the Escuela Militar,[7] but that at the moment they didn't have a vehicle, so I would have to wait. I told him that my wife and my mother were waiting in my car and that I could get to Escuela Militar on my own. He responded that that would be fine, and we agreed to do that. I remember that as I was leaving, there was a group of civilians and priests in the door of that office, who asked me to which party I belonged. When I said I belonged to the Izquierda Cristiana (Christian Left),[8] a priest come over to say an affectionate hello and wish me luck; he told me to have faith. I got the impression that the rest of the people also thought that everything would be cleared up relatively quickly and that the situation would soon normalize.

I went downstairs. Jorge Tapia and I signaled to the soldiers that we were leaving. Outside, my family was waiting nervously, especially my mother. They told me that after I had entered the ministry, one of the soldiers asked them what they were doing. When they told him that they were waiting for someone who had presented himself, he told them: "Oh, it's too late. He should have appeared right away. Now he surely will be shot."

We got in the car and drove toward Escuela Militar on our own. The atmosphere was very tense. The area was totally isolated, with soldiers and tanks all around. We moved slowly.

Along the way we chatted with Jorge Tapia. Neither of us knew what we were getting into nor what new stage of our lives we were entering. He told me that earlier that morning, his brother-in-law had left his house minutes before the curfew was lifted (on that day it was lifted at noon). He was arrested, brutally beaten, and, in a semiconscious state, dragged to a ditch in an upper-class neighborhood. When he regained consciousness, he discovered that he was lying on top of several dead bodies.

We stopped at Jorge's house to pick up a suitcase with some clothing and then we drove to Escuela Militar.

7. The Escuela Militar is Chile's West Point, where army officers are trained. During the coup d'état, it was a command center.

8. The Christian Left, Bitar's party, was composed largely of left-leaning Democrats who split from that party and joined Allende's Popular Unity coalition in mid-1971, nearly a year after Allende's election, in protest against the centrist Christian Democrats' electoral alliance with the Right.

Judging by the number of cars parked around the Escuela Militar, there were a lot of people there. Certainly many were family members of the junior officers in charge of security, bringing them food and changes of clothing. We got out of the car, each of us with a travel bag with what we would need for four or five days, corresponding to the expectations we had formed.

When I got out of the concentration camp after being held prisoner for more than a year, my mother told me that when we arrived at the Escuela Militar, I had told her that though I had no idea what was happening, I estimated that whatever it was could last a year or two. I don't remember having said that, but if it's true, it shows that the brain works on several planes, like two parallel minds: one cold and rational, situated outside of the subjective, and another, dominated by the way one wishes things were.

We said a tense good-bye, thinking that it would be for only a short time, but as if we knew inside that we were crossing the threshold to something much larger. At the moment we entered the Escuela Militar, a photojournalist ran toward us and took a picture. The photo appeared the next day on the front page of *El Mercurio* newspaper.[9]

A few minutes later, the atmosphere changed abruptly. We handed over our documents, which were never returned to us. The soldiers in charge, whose rank I couldn't identify, forced us to stand in different corners, without talking. They spoke with a dry and hard tone. Around the same time, a young man came in who had been detained under unknown circumstances. Soldiers forced him against the wall with his arms and legs spread. They hit him so he would spread them wider. He was insulted, pushed around, and brought inside the building.

We waited for half an hour while they took down our information. Right after that, in a much harsher tone, they brought us inside. We passed a kind of gymnasium where cadets were lying on the floor in combat positions. Some were joking; others were serious, as if it were a real combat situation.

We went to the top floor, to a large room adjacent to a terrace where there were many detained people. My first big surprise was to see several people who had been proclaimed or assumed dead or shot in the previous three days, such

---

9. *El Mercurio*, the flagship newspaper of the rightist Agustin Edwards, had led a media campaign against the Allende government that culminated in the coup. Declassified US documents have demonstrated its covert links to the CIA. It was one of two newspapers allowed to continue publishing after Allende's overthrow.

---

as Aníbal Palma[10] and Daniel Vergara.[11] I was happy to find them alive, despite these dire circumstances.

I imagined that their wives had no idea what they had been through and were probably very anxious worrying about their husbands.

As I entered, many people came over to hear news updates, since they had been incommunicado. At the same time they were happy to be reunited and alive. We broke into small groups and tried to find out what was happening.[12] I had spoken with Lucho (Matte) before turning myself in: he had had the same doubts and told me that he had been in contact with generals who were friends but hadn't received any definitive answer about what would happen to us.

We were all anxious. A TV was on and later we watched the replaying of the tragic bombing of La Moneda—the moment when a military car drove off and the announcer said that it carried the remains of Salvador Allende. We also saw José Tohá[13] as he was entering La Moneda just before the bombing, and when asked about the coup d'état, he said: "We are here. The people have elected Salvador Allende as president of the republic for six years. This govern-ment should have a duration of six years." They asked him, "What are you doing here, if this place is going to be bombed?" Tohá responded, "I came to be with the president. That is my responsibility."

Our mood was one of uneasiness and worry about not being able to contact our families. Some officers came in and said hello with a certain normalcy. We asked two military chaplains to keep our wives informed and to bring us news from our families.

10. Aníbal Palma was a leader of the leftist faction within the centrist Radical Party that remained in the Popular Unity coalition. As minister of education, he had pressed for an educational reform that included a uniform curriculum for private, public, and religious parochial schools. As a result, Palma was attacked by the opposition media and by the Popular Unity's opponents. He was a predictable prime target of the post-coup repression.

11. Daniel Vergara, the Communist Undersecretary of the Interior, was in charge of security during the Allende government. Detested by the rightist opposition, Vergara was another predictable target of the postcoup repression.

12. Bitar noted the presence of a number of elected officials, government ministers, and party leaders of Unidad Popular (Popular Unity Coalition) who were imprisoned on Dawson Island at various points in time, listed at the beginning of this book.

13. José Toha was a close friend and Socialist comrade of Allende who held several high positions in his government. He had been minister of the interior—in Chile, the top cabinet position—and had also been Chile's vice president and acting president when the president traveled abroad.

We stayed there from the day I arrived—Thursday, September 13, at 6:00 p.m.—until Saturday the fifteenth at noon. During that time, officers came over to tell us that they had found drugs and pornographic photos at Tomás Moro and Cañaveral.[14] Based on our relationship with the president, we knew this was false. We were shocked and outraged.

Later we had to form a line to go to bed: three or four to a room, no talking allowed, lights off, and with the rule that we weren't allowed to get close to the window. We rested on these beds, and during the night we withstood constant harassment from the soldiers who would come in and out clicking their heels, turning on the light, asking our names, shouting at us. Throughout the night we heard gunshots directed toward the outside as if they were fighting off an attack or preventing one.

That night Benjamín Teplisky[15] was put in my room, and later Héctor Olivares, a Socialist congressional deputy from Rancagua. Like me, both of them had appeared voluntarily before the military authorities. Hours later José Cademártori[16] came in—he had been detained at the house of party comrades in a suburb of Santiago.

The next day a very curious thing happened, revealing the ignorance among people in the new government about the goals that had inspired the coup leaders, who, I believe, were a minority within the armed forces. At around 10:00 a.m., we learned that the new minister of justice, Gonzalo Prieto, who had been sworn in with the new cabinet the night before, would soon visit us. At noon the minister appeared, accompanied by Undersecretary Max Silva. Nervously, with a cold amiability, he asked us to take a seat. He expressed his condolences for the death of President Allende and said that he understood the pain that we felt under the circumstances. Surprisingly, he then addressed us each as "Mr. Minister" and said, "I have come of my own volition, because this afternoon we have our first cabinet meeting and I would like to know your opinion about the possibility of your leaving the country."

There were diverse reactions because some, predicting that the situation could become more violent, saw the advantage of accepting the offer. However,

14. Tomás Moro and Cañaveral were residences of Salvador Allende. In Chile, the presidential palace houses his government headquarters and offices but is not the president's residence.

15. Benjamín Teplisky was a Radical Party leader and executive secretary of the Popular Unity coalition.

16. José Cademártori was a leading Communist economist and a congressional deputy.

the almost unanimous position was that everything would depend on the circumstances and developments of the following days. As members of the cabinet or senators and deputies of the legitimately elected Congress, we told him that we would be willing to be held accountable to the country for our political actions and our public lives. Mr. Prieto responded that he wanted to represent our perspectives in a more formalized way. If there were multiple concerns, we should present them in writing so that he could represent our position as accurately as possible. After several conversations in which various people requested to be freed immediately and to return to their homes, we agreed that Mr. Prieto should come the next morning around noon to pick up the written statement that we would draft.

The next day, Briones[17] and Almeyda[18] and one or two others worked on the document. Given the circumstances, we proclaimed our willingness to accept responsibility for our actions and remain in Chile, while leaving the door open so that if the situation became violent, we could consider the option of leaving the country. However, surprisingly, just moments before finishing the document to give it to the minister of justice, we received an overriding order to gather our belongings within five minutes and line up in front of our rooms. We did so, and they walked us downstairs.

In the meantime, something worth retelling occurred. Osvaldo Puccio, Allende's secretary, had been detained in the Ministry of Defense when he went to negotiate with the generals at the request of the president before the bombing. He was at La Moneda with his twenty-year-old son, a law student, who had accompanied his father that morning to take care of him because he had heart problems. At the ministry, the generals told Puccio: "Go back to La Moneda and don't worry about your son. We'll keep him here for a bit and then we'll send him home." However, after he was taken to the Escuela Militar, Puccio started to worry about his son; he learned he had never arrived home, not that day nor the twelfth, thirteenth, or fourteenth. He did everything possible to try to find his son, and asked that if they found him, they bring him to the Escuela Militar.

It happened at the exact moment that we were exiting the Escuela Militar— on Saturday, September 15, at noon—young Osvaldo Puccio Jr. arrived and lined up next to his father. He was wearing his clothing from the day of the

17. Carlos Briones, Allende's friend and fellow Socialist, was minister of the interior and thus vice president when the coup took place.

18. Clodomiro Almeyda was a longtime Socialist party leader and Allende's foreign affairs minister.

coup and a coat loaned to him by another detained prisoner at the Chile Stadium[19] where he had been taken from the Ministry of Defense. He insisted on not abandoning his father.

We lined up and boarded a bus. There the conditions changed radically. They brought all of us to the middle of the bus, which was filled with Escuela Militar cadets in their battle uniforms, with submachine guns and grenades. They made us lie down on the bus floor, one against the other. They told us that any movement that we made would be motive for them to shoot. They said that if anything unusual happened, our lives would be in danger and we could be shot.

The bus sped away, followed by other vehicles with armed men, and passed through much of Santiago, eventually heading toward Cerrillos Airport. It entered from the side and went to the Seventh Aviation Group of the air force. When we got there, we saw that the area was surrounded by a large number of armed men aiming their guns at us. The bus parked beside an airplane. They called us one by one, and with curses and insults they hurried us off the bus. When we stepped on the stairs to get off, they would give us a strong push, so that most of us stumbled off the bus and some fell. Uniformed men surrounded us. Some of them took the few belongings that we carried, threw them on the ground, and scattered them. Then they ordered us with insults to pick them up and get on the plane. They rebuked some people more harshly, saying, "So you wanted to destroy the country, asshole?" They pulled our clothing, tearing the buttons, and pushed us. A little ways off I could see a foreign officer, apparently Brazilian, observing this maneuver.

Among my belongings I had a notepad where I had written four or five pages during the two days that I was at Escuela Militar, describing what had happened and commenting on it. I was afraid that this could fall into the wrong hands, so the few observations that I made were written in a rather unintelligible handwriting, in English and French. These pages were pulled out and brought to one of the officers in charge, who tried to make out what was written and couldn't. He didn't call me up to explain and I was warned that I couldn't write another word.

19. The Estadio Chile (Chile Stadium) was a smallish indoor arena in downtown Santiago near the main train station and the Universidad Técnica del Estado (State Technical University). Like the more famous National Stadium, it was used as a concentration camp and center of interrogation, torture, and execution in the aftermath of the coup. It was there that the celebrated Communist singer-songwriter Víctor Jara was identified and executed. The stadium is now named after him.

We got on the plane. Again a man with a submachine gun at each end corralled us in the center. Everyone from Escuela Militar was there, except Carlos Briones. (Later we found out that he had been sent home under house arrest.)

We had felt the first violent shock—since the moment that we left Escuela Militar—of the realization that we could be facing death. We had felt this fear again on the bus, then again at the moment we boarded the plane. We had heard terrifying rumors of people being thrown into the sea from the air.

We knew we were heading south, because someone had overheard right before boarding that our destination was Punta Arenas. But nothing more.

In these sorts of situations, one lives in a state of relative unconsciousness, not knowing what threat or danger one faces; and if one does know, one can't entirely take it in. Simultaneously, one acts as if things were normal. I remember strange behaviors, like when Enrique Kirberg, president of the Universidad Técnica del Estado, started making a list on the plane of the things that he would be able to buy in Punta Arenas, because prices were lower there. The majority of us were taken aback at this but later we saw that this trait that characterized Enrique turned out to be very positive in the situations we were living: it was his optimism and ability to focus on mundane problems that allowed him to survive with less risk of mental instability.

The same thing happened when the minister of justice had visited us. We had debated about things that later made us laugh. For example, someone pointed out that he had meetings scheduled for that week and he had to cancel them, so they should let him out. Another insisted that he had to give classes on Monday, and asked that if he were not let out before that day, his students be notified.

The flight went on without delay until we landed in Punta Arenas around 10:00 p.m. Guns were pointed at us as we exited the plane down the small staircase. It was nighttime and the area was completely dark, so it was difficult to make out the figures surrounding us. The lights that illuminated the area were pointed at us and blinded us. Behind these lights I could see a row of hats, queued silhouettes of officers, watching the show: all of the ministers, senators, and congressmen from the government that they had just deposed.

We were held in pairs after getting off the plane. They took pictures of us and made us turn around, so that we couldn't see the faces of the officers. Then, corralled, we walked toward one side of the plane. There we approached two armored hatchback vehicles. Before getting in, they put hoods over our heads. I remember the feeling of drowning inside that hood, of going to an unknown place, oblivious to what was going on, while they shoved us into each other. After a while they closed the hatch and started the vehicle.

I confess that the feeling of terror was overwhelming. In total darkness, in a state of semi-asphyxiation and being pushed about on all sides, we heard an intense noise and a huge vibration. My sensation at that moment was that they were going to kill us, and later, when we were able to talk again, I confirmed that we had all experienced the same dread.

In the middle of the deafening shrillness, we continued to drive for forty-five long minutes. Where were they taking us? We only knew that we had landed at Punta Arenas. Would we be going to an army base in the area, close to the mountain range? Would they kill us in a wasteland? A wave of panic washed over us. Curiously, though, in the moments when I knew I could die, I had a sensation of calm. I felt that I was hanging from a thread, close to nothingness.

The armored vehicles stopped and the hatches were opened. We got out one by one. They took our hoods off. I was forced to walk without being able to see any of my companions. There was no one nearby. I climbed onto the deck of a barge and was brought through a real labyrinth. At every turn there was an armed marine. We went from this barge to another and another, until we arrived at one where I was led into a kind of storeroom, where I met up with the others.

We were brought there one by one, in absolute silence. Some were sitting, others standing, while armed sailors guarded the doors. When no more prisoners arrived, a young officer appeared, smiling, and spoke to us, mixing in some English words: "Okay, all right. Are we all here? Good. I want to warn you that here you must not speak, you must not converse, and you must not sleep. You should already know well enough that you must not move."

He left, came back, made another series of similar observations, left again. At that moment we realized that we were all there, except Daniel Vergara.

The harshness bordering on brutality of some of the officers from the different branches of the military contrasted with the deference of others. Many of them reacted normally in front of us. I remember that one approached Kirberg and started to talk with him—he wanted to be admitted to the Universidad Técnica del Estado and he asked Kirberg for advice, as president of the university, even under those circumstances.

After waiting for several hours, we started to feel a slight swaying of the barge and we left at about midnight. All of us were very sleepy. Aniceto Rodríguez[20] leaned on a table and dozed off. Suddenly an officer came over and hit him in the ribs with the butt of his gun, yelling: "You cannot sleep; it's forbidden!"

We were transported without speaking, without moving, and without sleeping throughout the night. At about six in the morning we felt the boat

20. Aniceto Rodríguez was a moderate Socialist senator and longtime party leader.

scrape the bottom: our vessel had stopped. We exited the cabin onto the deck and walked toward the side of the barge where a wide plank stretched to the shore.

This was the scene: snow on the ground, and a line of armed men. In front of us, large trucks with their lights spotlighting our faces.

Freezing air.

We had to cross this plank. It was Dawson Island, but we wouldn't know that until later.

Compingim

We got off the barge and carried our scarce belongings to a truck. They had already made Cademártori and Vergara climb into this vehicle. I was surprised to notice that Vergara's hand was bandaged, whereas in the plane he had been totally fine. We put our things in the truck while people continued to disembark one by one. There were many older people; the oldest was Julio Palestro, who was over sixty and had a damaged spinal column and kidney problems. He could hardly walk. He also had a serious case of diabetes, and on several occasions his physical health was in a critical state. As he picked up his luggage and started to walk down the plank, he couldn't keep his balance and he fell into the water with his bags. It was hard to imagine being in such frozen water at his age.

It was 6:00 a.m.

They had us walk single file and then march. Almost all of us were still wearing the clothing that we had used on the day of the coup, which was appropriate for September in the central part of the country but totally inadequate in this frozen Antarctic island: a light suit, shirt and tie, street shoes. To walk for several kilometers through snow at the austral dawn, surrounded by sailors with submachine guns, was a hallucinatory experience. Fortunately, a vehicle came to pick up the eldest among us. We walked like this for several kilometers until we came to a ravine in a corner of which we could see barracks made of shiny brass, their roofs covered with snow, surrounded by barbed wire. At first glance the structures were rudimentary: very light metal huts with gravel on the ground. There was a little stream, and snow. There was no hint of the basic conditions necessary for withstanding a long-term stay.

We entered one of the barracks, where we were settled and given a mug of coffee. Then, the commander of the naval base, Jorge Fellay, addressed us. We found out later that Fellay had been told of our impending arrival only hours earlier. He made us listen to his list of rules that we must follow as "prisoners of war." It was the first time that we had heard that we were "prisoners of war," and as such we were considered "generals" of the enemy army.

At this point we were all exhausted, after several intense days and strong emotions. Under these circumstances, everyone generates energies from wherever they can, even those who had suffered the most violence. Such was the case of Daniel Vergara, undersecretary of the interior at the time of the coup.

As I mentioned, when I put my things in the truck, I saw that Daniel's hand was bandaged. What had happened to him? When he got into the armored car, Vergara was pushed against the people around him, all of them hooded. When the tank started moving and they closed the hatch, the weapon of the soldier who was with them had slipped, hit the floor, and went off. With all the noise around, the shot wasn't heard. The bullet ricocheted off the metallic ceiling and was embedded in Daniel's hand. He didn't hear the shot either; he was hooded, constricted, and tense. He didn't even feel the pain. A bit later he noticed something warm and sticky running down his body. He saw that he was bleeding but didn't know from where. He told the soldier who was guarding them, and the soldier ordered him to shut up, since they couldn't do anything about it. He had to bear the forty-five-minute ride in the tank, bleeding. When they arrived at the destination, he got out and onto the barge. Once there, Vergara said he was wounded and they took him to a nurse who had him lie down on a tabletop and examined him. They found and sewed the wound on the spot, with no anesthesia and without removing the bullet, which they didn't notice was still inside him. When he got off the barge, they made him get on the truck and carry his own bags, with his hand in that condition.

That's how we found ourselves: exhausted, tense, and one wounded. It was dawn on Sunday, September 16, 1973. In that state we had to listen to the base commander dictate the rules we would be subject to. I don't remember all of them, but they were disquieting. We were told that if there were ever an attack on the island, we would be immediately shot. Any lack of discipline or disobedience of orders would be considered a war crime and therefore be punished by execution. We couldn't approach the soldiers or speak to them. Any contact with the officers had to be through a delegate who would deal directly with the commander. We couldn't come within three meters of the barbed wire.

At that point we weren't very aware of what was happening. We walked through the snow to one of the barracks and went inside. Finally, we were authorized to sleep until noon.

The barracks housed a series of bunk beds very close together. Between the rows of bunks, there was an aisle that was about thirty or forty centimeters wide, so that one had to turn sideways to pass through. There were thirty-two of us in these barracks—no more than forty-five square meters—with one small window hole. There was hardly any fresh air to breathe. We also didn't have anywhere to put our things, except for on the mattress at our feet or under the headboard. Each of us had just one blanket on top of the mattress that we threw on ourselves to sleep for a few hours.

Around the barracks there was a little patio, about twelve square meters, covered with gravel and surrounded by barbed wire. It was the only place where we had some minimal space to move around, and it faced the officers' and noncommissioned officers' (NCOs) offices.

In the days that followed, this was our living space. We were enclosed inside all day. When orders were called out, we had to get dressed and line up in less than five minutes.

At night no one could leave the barracks after 9:00 p.m. One of the officers who made us line up each night before locking us in coined a phrase that we'll never forget. He told us that under no circumstances were we allowed to open the door and go out, because should that ever happen, "he who appears shall disappear." For that reason, any bodily needs had to be suppressed. To urinate we had a big metal trash bin that we put behind the door, such that in order to open the door one had to move the bin and put it at the foot of the closest beds. So at night, one had to get down from the bunk, walk down the aisle in darkness, urinate in the bin in front of the others, and return to the bunk. One night somebody was suffering major stomach pain and he could neither get out nor call for help. He had to get on the bin and take care of necessities in front of all of us, with no ventilation, feeling this absurd humiliation on top of the pain.

We weren't the only prisoners on the island. When we arrived, there were already some other prisoners brought from Punta Arenas, and we were banned from seeing them, so that they wouldn't find out who we were. Any time they had to leave the camp in one direction or another that would require them to pass in front of our area, we had to quickly enter our barracks so that they wouldn't see us. When they were shut inside their barracks, we could go out again.

At the beginning, our presence there caused a lot of curiosity; so much so that the officers already settled there as well as others who came from Punta Arenas would stop on the other side of the barbed wire to stare at us.

Because of the incredible cold and our inappropriate clothing, we got used to walking very briskly in the patio, moving around so that we wouldn't freeze.

For them it was an attraction and we felt like animals in a zoo. Some of them even seemed to enjoy the spectacle.

🌿

On the day we arrived we slept until noon. Then they led us out of the barracks for lunch elsewhere. It was on that first outing on Sunday morning when José Tohá recognized the place: "We're on Dawson Island!" He had visited in August 1972 with Luis Matte, when the government had turned over this huge Chilean territory (1,400 square kilometers) to the navy, after the Agrarian Reform had expropriated it from a business that had huge amounts of land in the Magallanes Zone.

On the first night there was a simulated execution of other prisoners. We were awakened around 1:00 a.m. by terrifying gunshots. We were surprised, since we had just arrived on this remote island and didn't yet know that there were other prisoners besides ourselves. We heard machine gunfire, then silence: we heard them bring someone, give orders, and then shoot. There were simultaneous shots and then just one, as if it were the coup de grâce. Then, we heard sounds like a big sack being dragged and thrown into a truck. The motor was already running, next to our barracks, and it drove away. This scene repeated itself throughout that first night and the following night. Most of us thought that they could be shooting people from nearby Punta Arenas. Later we would learn from other prisoners from Punta Arenas that they had been subjected to the same drill. Not only that, but on the nights of the eleventh and twelfth, they had ordered some of the prisoners against the wall as if they would be executed, but their guns did not have bullets.

Two nights later, around 4:00 or 5:00 a.m., a noncommissioned navy officer came in and summoned Lazo and Schnake. They got dressed without knowing where they would be taken. Surely they thought they would be interrogated, but they never suspected all that they would suffer through, that they would go through the process that became known as the "Air Force Trials."[21] It was the last time they were seen on the island.

The following night while we were sleeping, two soldiers opened the door again and called out my name in the same way they had called for Schnake

21. Soon after the coup, the Chilean Air Force (Fuerza Aérea de Chile, FACh) began a relentless wartime prosecution of its own officers who were accused of having collaborated with the Allende government. Several civilians who worked in high public office—such as Lazo and Schnake—were also involved in these trials. The air force was the only branch of the military to undertake these internal prosecutions.

and Lazo; it filled me with worry, although I didn't know what I was in for. I went up to the watchman and he gave me a package from Kenny, my wife. At that moment I was filled with relief: it was nothing serious. On the contrary, this showed that now our wives knew where we were. I told the others right away: they had figured out where we were and they didn't give up until they found a way to send us clothing and food. Our wives' tenacity and perseverance during our time at Dawson would earn them the nickname Las Dawsonianas.

It's funny how the package ended up in my hands. When Kenny figured out where I was—through a friend of her parents who had connections in the Ministry of the Interior—she wanted to send me winter clothes. This friend told her that she could send me correspondence through the mail to the Third Naval Zone at Punta Arenas. She decided to send three packages with warm clothing. When she told the other wives, they laughed at her naïveté. However, I was the first person of the group to receive a letter and clothing, although one of the three packages never made it to me.

From the first lunch we had to make up a way to organize ourselves into groups that we utilized throughout our imprisonment; we called ourselves "ranchers": those in charge of the "rancho," or field kitchen. We divided ourselves into teams of four or five people that rotated each week, serving breakfast, lunch, and dinner, clearing tables, and washing dishes. We weren't allowed to enter the kitchen or use hot water, so we had to go to a freezing stream and use dirt, sand, or clay to rub the grease off the trays. I remember the first day that we had to do this, the first afternoon and evening, lined up next to the river under a moonless sky with no light. We knelt at the side of the stream where the snow-water froze our hands just long enough for each prisoner to rinse his own tray, and then the "ranchers" on shift that night would do the scrubbing.

Personal hygiene was another story. In the mornings they would blow a whistle or a bugle—or sometimes just bang on the door—to get us up; we would have between three and five minutes to leave the barracks and line up. During the first days, most of us slept in the clothes we had arrived in: we didn't have pajamas, sheets, or blankets. That way we were ready to leave right away whenever necessary. We would jump out of bed already dressed, throw a jacket on top, squeeze through the narrow aisle, and line up outside. The cold was penetrating. We had to stand there with our towels and, if one had them, a toothbrush or bar of soap. In groups of three we left the barbed-wire patio toward the stream, where we pulled on a rope attached to a bucket hanging from a tree branch. We would get more freezing water and empty it in two or three pulls. We barely had time to rinse our mouths with some toothpaste, splash our faces, dry off, and run back to the group to line up. The others had to wait their turns to run and repeat the scene.

After that we could ask permission to visit the latrines. These were tiny huts with a little door, and the waste flowed into the stream. At first we couldn't be in them without being watched, so any time that someone asked permission to go he had to leave the door open so that an armed man could watch over him. Later we had to build another latrine along the stream.

Something that was shocking, which we later communicated to the Red Cross when they came to inspect, was that another concentration camp was situated up-river from ours. Their kitchen and latrines flowed into the stream that we used to wash our dishes and ourselves with wastewater. Every day we would see excrement and waste flow past us, and we had to avoid them when we bathed.

A few days later, we were suddenly no longer allowed to use the barracks where our meals had been served. Instead they set up a tent outside within the fenced courtyard, on top of the rocks, snow, clay, and moisture, and that was our new mess hall. They brought our food there in big pots and pans, with soup or some stew. They would put them on big tables and we would use ladles to serve it into cups. Meanwhile, the "ranchers" would be waiting to pick up the dishes, wash them, and come back. The cold was unrelenting, and the older prisoners' health was quickly deteriorating.

We spent a good part of the first days in the patio, because we could only cross the barbed wire fences to eat, wash, or go to the latrines. Finally we were authorized to bring in pieces of wood so that we could make a bonfire. We would walk around and congregate by the fire. Later we progressed to using some empty cans to add handles made of wire through a hollow stick. This allowed us to have "mugs" for coffee to drink at night. A huge part of our lives revolved around the bonfires.

In the first few days, things took place that shocked us at first but became routine throughout our stay. One of them was the first search on the island. We had already suffered through searches at Escuela Militar, while getting on and off the plane, and arriving on the island. They confiscated pencils, lighters, wallets, money, watches, and so on. Now we experienced another search. The sailors or marines would enter the courtyard and aim at us, corralling us to a corner of the fences. Part of the fence was covered with planks so that we couldn't see the barracks of the prisoners from Punta Arenas. They lined us up against these planks. It was impossible not to be terrified when we were herded into a corner surrounded by armed men. More than once we thought they would shoot us. Then they would call us one by one. We had to raise our arms, put our head against the planks, legs apart. They kicked us to spread our legs wider, which made it easy to slip and scrape our hands on the barbed wire.

This type of search occurred many times and was always very tense. The purpose was to check if we had anything that could be used in an assault. They would examine our bodies to see if we had picked up any nails, wire, or anything that could be "dangerous" to the naval base.

Our belongings had been registered at the beginning, and we had practically nothing. What they really cared about, it seemed, was what we wrote, as we were prohibited to do so. During the first days, we had no paper at all. Our books had already been revised by naval intelligence to ensure that they didn't contain anything "subversive."

So we lived with constant tension. We were all very affected by Daniel Vergara's situation. Dr. Jirón had examined his hand shortly after arriving and discovered a foreign object—the bullet—lodged inside. It took him a lot of effort to be granted permission to speak with base commander Fellay and to convince him that Daniel urgently needed an operation. The officer didn't believe him, saying that at no time had any shots been fired. But Jirón insisted and finally Vergara was sent to a hospital in Punta Arenas. When he returned he came with a cast on his wrist, but Jirón saw that the bullet still had not been removed. Days later, thanks to Jirón's continued insistence, Vergara was sent again to Punta Arenas, where he was finally operated on. Throughout this time, Daniel suffered through intense pain, on top of the cold, but he did not complain, trying not to disturb us at night so that we could sleep.

This place, where we would stay until December 15, was called Compingim (Compañia de Ingenieros del Cuerpo de Infantería de Marina—Company of Engineers of the Marine Corps). We were under the direct orders of Fellay and a Lieutenant Barriga. Our group was called Sierra. Every prisoner was given a number, so that from that moment on I became Sierra-22.

We had to designate a delegate and a subdelegate, and we chose Edgardo Enríquez and José Tohá, two men of great moral, intellectual, and human quality.

Edgardo knew Fellay from before because he was a doctor and had risen to the rank of captain in the navy, to which he dedicated thirty years of his life. He had known Fellay in the navy as his student; this personal history made Fellay more compassionate, so that despite the situation, there was a basic level of respect, and we were permitted to organize some courses and talks.

That was one of the reasons why Edgardo Enríquez was chosen to be our delegate, a post that he later had to abandon due to a bitter argument with one of the noncommissioned officers about the work conditions and the treatment we received.

The commander took it upon himself to construct a "newspaper wall" soon after our arrival. Every morning around 11:00 a.m., having received the newspapers from Punta Arenas, he would post clippings with falsehoods about us, about what was happening, about the dead—there were lists of them— and stories of persecution that many people were subjected to. Besides this, we didn't have any other source of information. We were incommunicado.

On one of those afternoons, they brought a television set to the tent, at the time that the news aired. We saw a newsreel about the bombing of La Moneda, the president's death, and then a series of declarations by members of the junta about their plans for the future, which coincided on at least two points: to "eradicate the cancer of Marxism" and to remove all political parties in order to end the politicization of the country. Among that day's news, Admiral José T. Merino announced that they had found a large amount of money in the possession of Clodomiro Almeyda's wife, money that did not belong to them. This lie had a big impact on Clodomiro.

Later, another officer had to refute this accusation, recognizing that the money corresponded to income from the cafeteria at the Casa de Cultura Gabriela Mistral,[22] of which his wife, Irma, was director. As it was every weekend, the money had been stored in a bag in the cafeteria safe, the keys to which were in the hands of its director.

A week after our arrival, at around 5:00 p.m. while we were walking in the courtyard, we were rushed into the barracks as a truck approached. When we were allowed to go out again, we learned that another group of prisoners had arrived. We thought that it would be bringing people from Santiago, from among those we had seen at Escuela Militar or others who had been arrested earlier. But we were wrong. A bit later we saw seven people enter the concentration camp. I didn't know any of them.

22. The Casa de Cultura Gabriela Mistral functioned in the eponymous building, later renamed Diego Portales, and was headquarters of the military government until March 1981.

They were from Valparaíso: Leopoldo Zuljevic, former superintendent of customs, who was over sixty years old and had retired in 1972; Sergio Vuskovic, mayor of Valparaíso; Andrés Sepúlveda, deputy (member of Parliament); Max Marholz and Ariel Tacchi, municipal councilors from Valparaíso; Luis Vega, a lawyer from the Valparaíso regional administration; and Walter Pinto, an engineer and manager of the Ventana copper foundry.[23]

I remember their faces: they were terrified when they arrived. They had spent ten days—from September 11 through the twenty-first or twenty-second—on the *Esmeralda*, the navy's training ship.[24]

They told us how they had been removed from their homes after midnight on the eleventh and brought directly to the *Esmeralda*. There, according to their testimonials, they were stripped to their underwear, forced to lie on the deck of the ship or in the storerooms. They spent a long time lying face down on the floor with their hands behind their necks, being beaten. Every so often, they told us, some of them would be taken away for even more violent treatment: they would be tied to one of the galley poles and beaten on their stomachs and faces, and then freezing water was thrown on them. Others received electric shocks on their mouths, chests, and genitals. They spent the majority of their time on the ship subjected to these punishments. Their food was tossed on the ship floor, so they were forced to drag themselves over to eat it.

Under these conditions, they were brought to Dawson. Sepúlveda showed us his burnt tongue, eroded on the edges by the electric shocks. Marholz was urinating blood when he arrived, and one of his pelvic bones was smashed. Pinto had wounds on his back. Vuskovic had internal bleeding caused by all the blows to his stomach. He had also received electric shocks and they had rubbed salt in his wounds. Dr. Jirón had to examine each one.

The new arrivals were lodged with us. There weren't enough bunk beds, so they made the two-level beds into three-level beds, so that the people on the

23. Valparaíso was Chile's main port and third largest city, and served as Santiago's port. The city was the birthplace of the Socialist party and Allende's first political base. But Valparaíso was also the headquarters of the Chilean Navy and the starting point of the military coup that ousted Allende. It remained under naval control throughout the military dictatorship.

24. The *Esmeralda* was a four-masted brigantine, a sailing vessel purchased from Spain in 1951, and one of the "tall ships" in goodwill tours and commemorations. Its use as a torture center in the wake of the 1973 coup altered its image and its role. From that point on, its arrival at international ports was met with political protests.

top bunk couldn't sit up without hitting the ceiling. The overcrowding was getting even worse, as we were now forty-two people in forty-five square meters.

I don't know whether this harsh treatment was born out of hatred toward us, or because the sailors were obeying higher orders, or if it was a product of the tension that the sailors felt because of the responsibility of having the "generals of the opposing army" as their charges.

An incident that occurred shortly after our arrival is illustrative of this atmosphere. One evening the electricity went out. At that moment, some of us were walking toward the tent to have dinner. Others were already serving themselves. An alarm went off right away. With astonishing speed everyone from the camp—including the people in the kitchen—came running and surrounded us; aiming their guns at us, one gave the following order: "If anyone makes any movement while the lights are off, he will be shot on the spot."

I remember that some people had been about to sit, others had been walking in the aisle, others were ladling soup unto their plates. Hearing this, we were all petrified, because, as if that weren't frightening enough, he added: "This is our chance: whoever moves will be killed."

It wasn't a simple security measure, because we were on a practically uninhabited island controlled by the navy, surrounded by freezing water that no one could stand for more than five or ten minutes without freezing to death. Our group was composed mostly of older people, and it was completely absurd to think that this kind of measure and attitude originated simply out of a security precaution.

When we were in the courtyard, we were continuously observed like alien beings. When high-ranking officers visited, some of whom us prisoners had met under different circumstances in our lives—in official meetings or social gatherings when we were ministers, senators, or congressmen—they requested that we be locked in the barracks.

Another time, journalists from *El Mercurio* newspaper and other media arrived and took photographs that were published in the magazines *Vea* and *Ercilla*. These people observed us attentively. I don't know whether they were moved when they saw that in our country, people from the legitimate government were in a concentration camp behind barbed wire. The fact is that they came to photograph us, protected by armed men, without asking permission or excusing themselves, and they took pictures of us as if we were delinquents. We felt embarrassed and undignified.

We were also objects of curiosity. From the first weeks, planes left Punta

Arenas and came to "visit" us. The pilots flew as low as possible over the camp, dove down, did fancy turns, returned, all in order to get an aerial view of the place where the leaders of the Popular Unity government were confined.

After a fortnight of being enclosed in this courtyard, they took us out for a walk. I clearly remember this first time. We could walk, stretch our legs, breathe fresh air, and see the ocean, the trees, and the open fields. And so we walked, marching like a battalion.

Little by little our tasks became more routinized. Forced labor was part of our program from the beginning. This work would fluctuate—there would be more moderate times, and also very difficult cycles.

We were divided into work teams of ten men—at first "volunteers"—who were assigned specific tasks. Later, forced labor was mandatory and only the people for whom physical labor was practically impossible because of their physical condition—heart conditions, back problems, old age—could exempt themselves.

Once the groups were organized, we would line up at 8:00 a.m. We would board the trucks (called *logísticos*), in which the Engineering Company (Compingim) usually carted around sand, dirt, or other materials. There weren't any other vehicles, so the group of "volunteers" had to climb up the sides of the truck, holding on to the tires and jumping into the mud or other material piled up in the truck. The truck followed a path along the coast that connected Puerto Harris with the landing strip. Every once in a while we would stop to drop off a squad that was guarded by naval personnel or marines.

One of the jobs that we did was erecting electrical poles along this path, about twenty or thirty kilometers long. The task consisted of installing poles every fifty meters. We carried spikes, rams, and shovels, and dug holes about a meter deep and fifty to sixty centimeters wide. Then we would carry the heavy wooden poles, about six to eight meters long. We would stand them up and bury them in the holes, then pack in rocks and dirt to secure them. Usually the earth was very hard and rocky, and we would spend hours picking at the surface just to advance a few centimeters.

In the beginning when we hadn't yet received the clothes that we had asked our wives to send, we got blisters on our hands, and because of the density of the earth and the hard work that we weren't yet accustomed to, some people experienced dislocated wrists, pulled muscles, or simply strong pain in their arms and backs.

Each shift lasted a full day. It was cold and windy. Dawson is further south than the Falkland Islands;[25] in the northern hemisphere the equivalent latitude is in Siberia or Alaska, where by coincidence there is also a region called Dawson. At that time of year, the earth was still wet from the rains or the melting frost. When we found a dry place to rest, or if there was a downed trunk, we would make a bonfire to warm up. We usually ate on the ground. We worked from morning until noon, when a truck would come by and drop off some lunch—soup or beans or lentils—and some bowls. We would look for somewhere to eat where we could take refuge from the winds. An hour later we would take up the work again, until about five thirty in the afternoon, when the truck would come back to pick us up and bring us back to camp.

We returned exhausted every day. The only thing we had to look forward to then was the possibility of a letter with news from our families.

At the same time as the majority of us carried out this work—especially the younger prisoners—others stayed at the camp, fixing it up. They built our latrines over the riverbed and also some little canopies over the patio, to protect us from the rains and to give us the illusion that they could also protect us from the cold. So we made an effort to improve the only places where we could move about, because inside the barracks it was impossible.

Whatever the work consisted of, it was carried out without interruption, under any climatic condition except for torrential rain. When there were no trucks to bring us to our posting task, we would walk there. There were times when we had to walk five kilometers there and back. Sometimes we had to make this trip twice a day: morning and afternoon, carrying the tools home. Another frequent task was chopping firewood, which we needed for our bonfire in the camp and for the officers and noncommissioned officers (NCOs, or Non-Coms) in the kitchen.

During the first months in Compingim, two or three new tasks were added to the ones we were already working on. We called one of them "going quarrying." We would go in the truck to different places along the beach where there were big, round stones that we had to choose and put in the vehicle until the truck was full. Then they were taken to the commander's house in Puerto Harris. The stones were used to construct a wall around his garden.

Other times we would go "searching for peat." In some very humid areas, a layer of moss forms that rots after a few years, swamping the area. Our job was to gather all the rotten moss, pass it through a sieve, put it in bags, and leave them along the edge of the path, where a truck would pick them up later

25. The Falkland Islands are known in Spanish as the Islas Malvinas.

to use as fertilizer. In order to carry out this task, we had to get knee-deep in a swamp, sometimes with boots that the military officer in charge lent us or with our own shoes. Either way, we would leave smelly and covered in dirt.

I remember the mornings vividly, the moments when we would set about our tasks, trying to forget what we were living through. We would come back in the afternoons, looking for anything to calm our hunger or something warm to comfort us. We would lie on our mattresses to rest, waiting for the call to dinner.

We were always accompanied by conscripts or a noncommissioned officer. Among the former there were different attitudes. Some acted with equanimity. Others, surely selected for this kind of work because of their personalities, acted with rudeness and violence.

Here's an anecdote that illustrates a spontaneously gentle but dangerous attitude of a soldier, which happened soon after our arrival. One afternoon we were returning from our work and some beautiful geese were flying over us. Sometimes the conscripts would hunt and cook them. That day, one of them invited me to take some shots and he passed me his automatic weapon. I took a few unsuccessful shots and gave him back the gun. A few weeks later, that scene seemed absurd: if an officer had seen me with a weapon, he could have accused me of attacking the guard, with dire consequences.

In contrast, I had a totally different experience with another marine. He was short with mongoloid features. He was violent and impetuous, screaming at everyone that he was in charge and had to be obeyed. The first day he led a group of prisoners to work at a rigorous pace, imposing deadlines for every task. People complained about the demanding pace, pointing out the physical state of some of our fellow prisoners. In the afternoon he took out another group, which I was part of. We had to stand a certain distance from one another against the brush and he told us: "I will not accept any complaints, and anyone who expresses discontent will face the consequences. Things will be tough. You need to obey me and do exactly as I say."

We worked in holes filled with water, emptying them out with our hands to put in the poles. He imposed new work conditions: more than once he entertained himself by aiming at us with his machine gun, one by one for long periods, to see our reaction.

Then he decided that we should sing. We had to learn a series of military songs on the way to and from the worksite, carrying our tools on our shoulders and marching to the rhythm of the song. When we got close to the camp—or if we passed any officers or NCOs—we had to sing louder and tighten our march, to show off to the others. Later we learned that this officer had a nickname that the other marines gave him: Malacueva.[26]

One day Malacueva asked us what song we all knew, so that we could sing on the way to the site. Somebody suggested "Himno Americano," which names all the countries in Latin America. One of the last verses says: "Salvador, Cuba, and Panama are sovereign brothers of liberty." When we got to that part, Malacueva barked at us to shut up. He stopped the line and said: "Cuba shall not be named; nobody can sing the name Cuba, so when you get to that part of the song, take out that word."

And that's how, trying to contain our laughter, we started again and replaced the word Cuba with "mmmmm": Salvador, mmmm, and Panama are brothers, and so on." Malacueva also liked us to sing the hymn of the armed forces. When he taught us the words, he said: "In a copper of old gold."

Jaime Tohá corrected him: "Actually, it should say, 'In a coffer of old gold.'"

"Have you never been to Chuquicamata?"[27] retorted Malacueva, annoyed. "There the copper comes out with gold and that's why the song says, 'In a copper of old gold.'"

And that's how we had to sing it.

Because of this ritual of singing as we came and went, Jaime Tohá earned the nickname Pañuelito (Little Handkerchief). Every time that we were made to sing "Lili Marlene" and we got to the final verse (*"Adiós*, Lili Marlene"), Jaime, in the last row, would take out a white handkerchief and shake it, as if saying an imaginary good-bye to the song's protagonist. This was especially funny to us because those in charge never noticed this joke.

After a while, Malacueva was transferred because our complaints revealed the danger we were in under his watch. By coincidence, during the time that Dr. Jirón was working out of a little office in Puerto Harris to tend to the families of the officers, Malacueva had to respectfully serve him tea every morning at 10:00 a.m.

Another noncommissioned officer with special characteristics was one that they called Caballo Loco (Crazy Horse, some called him in English). He was a marine who was a good person but rather scatterbrained. On September 24 when we woke up, the flag was at half-mast. We were surprised, and because

26. Malacueva is a Chilean slang word meaning "tough luck."

27. Chuquicamata is the world's largest open-pit copper mine, located in northern Chile.

we couldn't think of any event that justified this, we started to speculate about something that might have happened that could change our luck. We asked Carlos Jorquera to find out. So he approached Caballo Loco: "Why is the flag at half-mast, sergeant?"

"Because a very important man has died."

"Who?"

"I don't know; I think it's a famous musician."

"A musician," said Jorquera, surprised. "What musician?"

"I think his name is Neruda."[28]

The food we received during this first part of our stay was relatively decent. Later, it really deteriorated, especially when we were brought to the concentration camp that was built especially for us. At Compingim, the food consisted of a *café con leche* and a bread roll in the morning before going out to work. At lunchtime we received a cup of something warm—broth or stock—and a plate of rice, potatoes, beans or lentils. About once a week we were given a piece of meat.

In the afternoons around 5:00 p.m., we would have a cup of tea and a roll. Dinner was the same as lunch, and there was a constant scarcity of vegetables and fruits, which meant a serious dietary deficiency.

We subsisted on this food at the beginning without major problems, despite the fact that it was inadequate considering the work pace we were subjected to. Our weight loss in the first months was considerable. Also, because we could only wash the dishes in the dirty water of the stream, it was easy to catch bacterial infections.

On rare occasions there was an exception to this nutritional regimen. On September 18,[29] for example, we were having lunch in the tent while a group of soldiers and an officer were served a special meal. Unexpectedly they brought over five empanadas for us to split among ourselves.

From the outset, those who were also trained as doctors took charge of our health. It was very reassuring to have Doctors Jirón and Guijón. Dr. Arturo Jirón was increasingly needed to tend to prisoners who arrived in poor condition from Punta Arenas as well as the military personnel and their

---

28. Pablo Neruda, the great Chilean poet, won the Nobel Prize in 1971. He was also a diplomat and a politician. He died twelve days after the military coup, on September 23, 1973, in Santiago. His death is still being investigated.

29. Chilean Independence Day is September 18.

---

families. This work as "official doctor of Dawson Island" had a curious begin-ning. One morning we were lined up singing the national anthem when the flag got all tangled on the flag post due to the strong winds. An officer sent a conscript to climb up the mast and release it. He climbed up, and after he was done he slid quickly down the pole. He didn't realize that there was a hook where the cord was usually wrapped. He suffered a major tear and fainted as he fell to the ground. He was taken to the nurse's quarters and when they took off his clothes they saw that his testicular sac had ripped open. Seeing this spectacle overwhelmed the practicing nurse. They asked for a doctor and found Arturo, for whom, as an expert surgeon, this seemed a simple operation in order to restore the original condition of the genitals. He proceeded imme-diately: "Do you have local anesthesia, nurse?" he asked.

"Yes, surgeon."

"Sutures?"

"Yes, surgeon."

He operated successfully, and from that moment on, Jirón began to be respected as a medical doctor, and as such was requested even after a full day's work.

The difficult access to the island meant that only one barge, boat, or plane arrived each week. Our doctors put forth the urgency of treating Daniel Vergara and getting him to the hospital at Punta Arenas, so that his hand wouldn't worsen. Similarly, Julio Palestro, who had diabetes, needed to be transferred to the hospital before he suffered a shock after his blood-sugar level increased dramatically, given the starchy diet.

When the sick arrived at the hospital, the doctors recognized their critical state and tended to them; but as soon as they showed any sign of improvement, the officers in charge would send them back to the island, where the cycle began again.

About a month after our arrival at Dawson, the Red Cross visited for the first time, without advance warning. The day before their arrival we were told that we could play soccer as part of a sports program. We were surprised at this nice gesture. Two or three of the friendlier officers approached us to let us know that they would put us in better quarters; they had reha-bilitated another barracks so that we could spread out a bit. The forty of us were split into a new barracks that was partitioned in two: one area was ten square meters and the other about four meters wide by eight meters long; another barracks was about four meters wide and five or six meters long. We baptized the three new zones as "Sheraton," "Tupahue," and "Valdivia," names of well-known hotels in Santiago.

It was a huge relief. It's incredible how under dire circumstances one is able to appreciate and placate oneself with so few things and small changes. The idea of having a bit more space, of being twelve people in an area of thirty square meters, in two-level bunks and with a wide aisle to circulate among them; the idea of being able to hang our things on a nail on the wall, or to put our bag under our bed, had been unthinkable when we were so overcrowded. The ability to move around and talk in a larger space produced a sudden change in our lifestyle. And then on top of that, we were told: "Gentlemen, we are going to give you sheets." They gave us ten sets and we decided that the eldest people would use them.

All this occurred, without our knowing it, the night before the Red Cross was to arrive. I remember it clearly because it was a moment of huge change for us. We allowed ourselves to hope that it had a greater meaning or was a sign of something better to come. We were always interpreting and assigning meaning to every unexpected detail. In every occurrence we would find some hope to cling to that would help us survive.

That's how the group got sheets, which we later had to abandon because we didn't have any soap or hot water to wash them. During our eight months at Dawson, we slept in these dilapidated bunks with dirty mattresses and a pair of blankets that were insufficient to fend off the unbearable cold. The mattresses were so lumpy and the springs so worn out that we had to put planks of wood under them so that our backs wouldn't ache. Later, the Red Cross sent us new blankets that, along with our jackets, ponchos, and other warm clothing, were heavy enough to get us through those freezing nights.

The next day they took us out to play soccer. We were happy to run, jump, and relieve stress. But the game went on for too long and we didn't know why. After three hours, exhausted by running around the field, we understood: a vehicle arrived and a group of foreigners got out—primarily Swiss, who introduced themselves as members of Red Cross International—and started to talk with us. Logically, the game had gone on so long so that the visitors could see us practicing a sport.

The first meeting with the Red Cross delegation basically consisted of identifying all the detainees. They verified whether everyone on their list was present, and checked if there was anyone else not on their list. We asked them about our *compañeros* who had been at La Moneda at the time of the bombardment of the palace, as we hadn't heard what had happened to them after. Months later we learned that many of them had died immediately following the coup.

The Red Cross confirmed conditions at the camp and learned that they had only improved the night before. They went through the barracks and latrines, saw how we washed and ate, the lack of ventilation or shelter from the cold. After a while we had become accustomed to the place where we lived and our basic necessities had been reduced to surviving and hearing from our families. We had lost the capacity to consider our lifestyle objectively. But for people coming from outside, the contrast was shocking and impressive.

We complained to them about the lack of contact with our families. We told them that we didn't know how long this would last, what they were accusing us of, whether we would be brought to trial, and whether we could rely on any form of legal defense.

After these first conversations, we returned to the camp. The officers in charge had been anticipating these visitors and they showed them around the camp with a lot of pomp. They were all in their dress uniforms. Later we found out that the official story told to the Red Cross was entirely different: that our food was the same as that of the soldiers and officers, with menus that didn't exist; that we were warm enough; and that labor was not forced but rather it was voluntary, only for those who chose to work, and a good way for us to distract ourselves.

Thanks to the Red Cross, we obtained permission to write home. From then on, we were allowed to send a letter to our families on Saturdays. We sat in the tent where we ate, and they gave us each a sheet of paper and five pencils that we had to rotate through forty prisoners. Writing letters on Saturdays became a weekly ritual. Once we were done, the delegate had to count the pencils and pages we had used, since we weren't allowed to keep them.

Because of the censorship, we chose our words carefully. Otherwise the letters wouldn't be forwarded because they were submitted to censorship at three points: first on the island, then at Punta Arenas, and finally in Santiago. The letters that we received had gone through the same scrutiny. I remember that a long time passed before we received the first responses from our wives. When they wrote, they didn't mention whether they had received our letters, so we didn't know if they had arrived. Sometimes the letters seemed like a dialogue of the deaf and dumb, without the ability to communicate with the other. The letters arrived after much delay, blacked out and cut up. On our end, we couldn't communicate our feelings, because they would surely be ridiculed by the censors, who sometimes added sarcastic comments next to what we had written.

Since we could normally only use one page, we began to develop a particular way of writing: our handwriting became smaller and smaller in order to take advantage of the one page. As time passed, the system was perfected, and many times a couple of our pages were the equivalent of six or seven in a normal letter.

A month after arriving, we received the first visit from official interrogators: two prosecutors in navy uniforms. According to some of the prisoners at Dawson from Punta Arenas who knew them, one of the lawyers was a Christian Democrat sympathizer. The man had a deferential attitude in the interrogations and subtly made known his dissent with some actions of the military junta that were coming to the surface.

One morning they came to get Puccio Sr., then Jorquera, and then Jirón and Guijón. They were blindfolded inside the barracks and led away, so that they wouldn't see their interrogators. The objective was to question them about what had happened at La Moneda on the day of the coup.

The description they gave the interrogators matched what they had already told us: early in the morning of Tuesday, September 11, 1973, President Allende received intelligence that the uprising would take place. In the middle of the night, the news coming from Valparaíso was that strange movements were happening in the navy. The president had called General Pinochet (recently named by Allende himself as commander in chief) to alert him, and to thank him for the level of commitment that he and other senior officers had displayed. Apparently, Pinochet had told him not to worry, that he had everything under control.

The president knew what was brewing and from that moment until he decided to go to La Moneda at 7:00 a.m., he continued to receive accounts of alarming news from Valparaíso.

His permanent advisors, journalist Augusto Olivares and medical doctor Danilo Bartulín, also went to the government palace. Then the ministers began to arrive—Palma, Jaime, and José Tohá.

When Allende arrived at La Moneda, his aides were already there but later left under his orders. Two or three Carabinero (national police) generals who were ousted by General César Mendoza[30] were also with Allende and let him know that they had lost control of the situation. They stayed by his side.

The president continued to receive updates. He called Pinochet to clarify the situation. But Pinochet had pivoted and ordered him to surrender. The

---

30. Mendoza became commander of the Carabineros on the day of the coup, after the seven most senior generals refused to betray their oath of loyalty to the elected president. Mendoza remained a member of the ruling military junta until August 1985, when he was forced to resign as a result of flagrant public human rights abuses.

president responded that he would not give up, and as president of the republic he asked the generals to come to La Moneda. They refused and threatened to bomb the presidential palace.

Then there was a series of telephone calls and comings and goings. Tohá and Briones tried to intervene, asking the *golpista* generals to wait, that they not provoke a massacre or a bombardment. But apparently those responsible for the uprising were fearful that if the situation were prolonged, they could lose the advantage they had gained with a surprise attack. They decide to move forward and bomb the palace.

Besides the president and some of his aides and ministers, various secretaries, administrators, and bodyguards were also inside La Moneda. It was easy to predict that blood would be shed, so several medical doctors were called to the palace, including Patricio Guijón. It was his first time at La Moneda; when he arrived around 9:00 a.m. the doors were locked, and he was let in only after much insistence that he had been summoned in case of emergency.

In the face of these bomb threats, Allende ordered the guards and police defending the palace to leave. By that time he was aware that there would be a coup d'état. Ever a man of principle, Allende wanted to avoid bloodshed and a civil war. At that point the attack began on the ground, with tanks and heavy arms. When there was a pause, the president ordered that all women leave the palace, including his daughters, Isabel and Tati, the latter eight months pregnant. They were able to escape before the aerial bombing. He also asked the ministers to leave, but most of them remained to show their support and decided to stay with Allende to the end. The president then addressed the country by radio. He told people not to go out into the street to defend the government. He knew that this would provoke a massacre of workers and of women and children. When he concluded his address, he decided to remain in the presidential palace, alone except for those collaborators who would not leave his side.

With this increasingly tense situation, it was impossible to negotiate or to have a dialogue. The aerial bombing was about to take place, and Allende had already ordered many people to leave, but others had remained with him. From among the supporters still with him within the palace, he sent a group out to parley. The group, including Puccio and his son and Flores, exited La Moneda carrying a white flag. They went to the Ministry of Defense across the Alameda boulevard and reached the group in operational command, which included, among others, Admiral Carvajal, later the minister of foreign relations, and General Nuño, later named vice president of CORFO. The officers warned that the timing was urgent: there was no possibility of negotiation;

the president must surrender. They also warned Allende's emissaries that they would "pay for what they had done." Fernando Flores in particular was threatened, warned that he was responsible for everything. It was impossible to delay any further or to arrive at any sort of agreement. The ultimatum was confirmed.

The group returned to La Moneda to communicate this response, but Allende had already made the decision that he would face what might come, to the very end. He had already made known that he would never go into exile nor would he be a nomad abroad while such tragic events happened in his country. So those who knew him best had no doubt what the course of events would be. For this very reason, the president himself was perhaps the calmest among them.

The bombing began, and some people—including the Tohá brothers and Almeyda—were able to take refuge in the basement of the Ministry of Foreign Relations, in the southern section of the palace. Others stayed with the president, including various medical doctors. Those who remained would later recount the terrifying experience of hearing the planes approach and feeling the bombs dropping and the buzzing sound as they fell. Then came the boom and the aftershocks, so similar to those of an earthquake. Then another buzzing sound and another tremor, over and over until the pilots launched their incendiary rockets. Then smoke and flames.

The suicide of Augusto Olivares, a close press advisor to the president, occurred during the bombing. Conscious of what was happening, Olivares walked toward the cafeteria on the first floor of La Moneda and with his revolver shot a bullet into his brain. Someone heard the gunshot and fetched Guijón, but Olivares was already near death. Dr. Guijón called Dr. Jirón over, but Olivares died in his arms. La Moneda was completely isolated. All the men in uniform had left, and there was no gunfight. Only a few close associates remained with the president, among them Arsenio Poupin, the undersecretary of government; Eduardo Paredes, director of Policía de Investigaciones (the Chilean FBI); Dr. Enrique Paris, educational advisor; Dr. Jorge Klein; sociologist Claudio Jimeno; Enrique Huerta, the administrator of La Moneda; Jaime Barrios, former president of the Central Bank; and others—no more than thirty—including the doctors and the president's personal bodyguards.

The fire began to spread and the bombardment continued. The smoke was suffocating. They had only one gas mask, which they passed around, each one using it for a few seconds of relief. The Gallery of Presidents was completely destroyed. The fire approached the area of the presidential offices and advanced toward the cabinet meeting room. Someone moved Chile's 1810 Declaration of Independence document to a safe place.[31] With its windows broken and its statues of former presidents knocked to the ground, La Moneda was in flames. Chile's entire tradition of independence and democracy had been crushed. The president ordered that those around him surrender and evacuate. He told them, "Begin exiting. I'll be behind you." They improvised a white flag made out of one of the doctor's white coats tied to a broom. When they waved the flag out the window, it was destroyed by a barrage of bullets. Then the gunfire stopped.

Apparently the phones were still working, because some ministers were able to call their homes. Someone communicated with the commanders of this one-sided battle, to tell them of the surrender. They started to exit through the Hall of Presidents toward the stairway that leads down to the entrance of La Moneda. The president stayed behind and went into the great salon near the dining room.

That was where the most tragic event of all took place, lived and related by Dr. Guijón to all of us at Dawson. Sometimes strange thoughts enter one's mind at critical moments. Guijón remembered that it occurred to him to bring home the gas mask to show his children as a remembrance of the bombing. At the moment that he returned to fetch it, he passed before the doorway of the Great Salon and saw a flash.

He looked into the room and saw President Allende sitting on one of the armchairs near the door, leaning to one side with a gun in his hands and his face deformed. Guijón approached him, but the president was dead. Guijón removed the weapon and stayed next to him, holding him up. Guijón believes a few minutes passed, though he didn't really have a notion of time at that point, until the soldiers entered La Moneda led by General Javier Palacios, who realized what had happened, took charge of the situation, and, after writing down his name, ordered Guijón out of the building.

What we know from then on is what the censored television news broadcasted: the same takes over and over again showing the group of firemen with the president's body wrapped in a blanket and then a truck driving away from La Moneda, carrying his corpse.

Some people present at the time told of the last group to leave La Moneda, who were beaten with rifle butts and taken to Morandé Street, where they were forced to lie facedown with their hands behind their heads. They couldn't talk or move. They were warned that if they made the slightest movement,

31. The document was later found and destroyed by a soldier in the attacking force.

they would be riddled with bullets. Then a group of soldiers began shooting over their heads.

Those who were present—and who later became my fellow prisoners—describe feeling at that moment that their only chance for salvation was death. Receiving the blows, hearing the bullets flying over their heads, having survived the bombing, knowing that the president had died, and being aware of the massacre that was unfolding around them and that would continue in the future made death appear to be the only exit. The president's staff, doctors, and body-guards were beaten right there on the ground. The most well-known ministers were taken from La Moneda and brought directly to Escuela Militar, including Almeyda, Briones, and the Tohá brothers.

General Palacios, in charge of the military attack on La Moneda, asked any medical doctors to identify themselves. Several did. "Gentlemen," said Palacios, "you may go to your homes, because you are here in a professional capacity, as am I."

Dr. Patricio Arroyo explained that there were other doctors there, lying in the street, and asked permission to go get them, but Palacios said it was too late. Arroyo waited and insisted, and finally was authorized to call the rest. Jirón, Bartulín, and Oscar Soto heard the call. Paris and Klein didn't hear it. When the group left its post, a fireman recognized Arturo Jirón and told Palacios, "This doctor was minister of health!" Palacios ordered them to take Jirón to the Ministry of Defense.

What happened to the group that stayed behind? It was not known at the time.[32] They all disappeared: doctors, sociologists, workers, an undersecretary of government, the president's personal bodyguards, a former director of Policía de Investigaciones.[33] Their families didn't know their whereabouts, and days later they learned that some of them had died. One of the most dramatic cases was Claudio Jimeno, a sociologist who worked at La Moneda. After he left the palace in a large group, no one ever heard from him again. His wife, Isabel Chadwick, left no stone unturned searching for clues of his whereabouts. For several months, she was told that he had been detained at an army base in the

32. After the dictatorship ended, the Truth and Reconciliation (Rettig) Commission was appointed by President Patricio Aylwin to establish what had happened to the disappeared and executed. It found that those close associates who had stayed with Allende until the end were taken from La Moneda to the Tacna regiment in the south of Santiago and executed.

33. Policía de Investigaciones was the Chilean equivalent of the Federal Bureau of Investigation.

Compingim

south, and so she sent money, clothes, and food. Later she learned that Claudio had died immediately after the military coup.

On that same morning that the interrogators came to Dawson, we learned that the rest of the people who ended up at Escuela Militar had lived very different experiences. Daniel Vergara, for example, was detained at the Ministry of the Interior and brought to the Ministry of Defense. They locked him in a room and two officers beat him. He was stripped, forced to kneel and stay like that, slumped, naked, for a long while. Then a more senior officer appeared, saw the situation, and asked his subordinates to leave. He told Vergara to get dressed, and then later sent him to Escuela Militar. Defense minister Orlando Letelier's experience was different: according to what he told us, he went to the Ministry of Defense with his chauffeur, a soldier. When he arrived, he got out of the car and was told that he wasn't allowed to enter. At that moment, his own driver aimed a gun at him and he was brought from the Ministry of Defense to the Tacna Regiment. He was locked in a dark room where he heard the sounds of people being brought in and beaten, shouts of desperation, and gunfire.

Meanwhile at Compingim, and in the time before we were sent to the new camp, life began to stabilize. We continued to work in eight-hour shifts, and were fed the same kind of food.

We never lost hope that there would be a relatively quick resolution to our situation. We constantly told each other that the following week or very soon we would receive good news, because we assumed that keeping us isolated from the world and incommunicado was unsustainable in the long run and that the junta had to arrive at some decision soon.

Later, when we got access to a shortwave radio, we heard about the constant attention paid to our group of Dawson Island prisoners by people in other parts of the world, and that lifted our hopes that we would be released soon. Some people thought that we wouldn't get out until Christmas, and we considered them pessimists. How could they even imagine that we would still be at Dawson at Christmas! Others thought that there would be some kind of resolution by the end of October. And we thought they were being negative, too. We were always stoking the idea of a way out, and that's what helped us bear our dire conditions. We tried to look beyond the tragic elements of our situation and to consider it a sort of adventure—or a collective nightmare—that we were going through and would soon transcend.

In the interim, the situation with the mail began to stabilize. They began to allow us to send and receive correspondence and packages with some regularity. The first set of correspondence from our wives arrived at the end of October. They informed us that they sent us warm clothing, thick shoes, work gloves, scarves, and heavy jackets that helped protect us from the cold climate. They also sent some food items that provided a welcome change. Later we learned that the majority of things never reached us.

Once a week we could send our letters, but they could not exceed one page, nor could they touch on virtually any theme other than a brief reference to one's personal condition and some inquiries about one's family. Because of the censorship, they received pages more than a month later with many words blacked out, sometimes even cut out with scissors. We also paid close attention to the letters we received, a month or a month and a half after they had been sent. When they got to us, they were so blacked out and cut up that we would have to shake the envelope to get all the little pieces out; they would be missing whole sentences and any sign of affection, especially at the closings. If our wives listed the enclosures they were sending with the letters, when they got to us the descriptions were blacked out with ink.

At the end of November and December, when they sent us some money so that we could buy some products directly from Punta Arenas, the amounts of money in the letters were blacked out. We later learned the real amounts our wives had sent; this was extremely costly for families without a decent income who had made a great effort to be able to send the funds to Dawson.

Our concern for our wives and children was well founded. Shortly after being detained, we learned that our families' economic situations had worsened. Our bank accounts had been frozen, funds retained, and our salaries cut. In my case I was suspended from my job at the University of Chile, where my salary was cut off due to "failure to come to work." My wife was told that she had to resign from her post at the National Health Service, because she was my spouse. My family and Kenny's joined together to support us financially, but most detainees were not so fortunate.

Meanwhile, the wives in Santiago and Valparaíso suffered through uncertainty and harassment by the officers in charge of political prisoners. During the first few months, letters and clothes were sent through an office at Escuela Militar. Our wives had to go there and hand over photos, addresses, and other personal information. Then in October they were placed under house arrest. They could receive visitors, but they couldn't leave their homes. After a while they were summoned back to Escuela Militar, where General César Benavides told them that their house arrest was being lifted, and that from that moment on his "protection" over them would also cease. Later they went through the Cendet (Centro de Enlace de Detenidos/Center of Links to the Detained), which was run out of the congress building. Their lives revolved around seeking information about their husbands; they were misled, rejected, and often rudely body-searched.

In the early days we weren't allowed to read. Toward the end of October this changed, and some of the books that our family and friends in Chile and abroad sent to us were permitted in the camp. The books were censored, and no social science titles were let in. They also prohibited books by famous authors associated with struggles for peace or liberty.

The case of Bertrand Russell was typical. His *Complete Works* were outlawed for a long time. Only after we insisted that Russell was actually a mathematician were his books permitted. There was no understanding that *Complete Works* didn't refer to one particular author, rather to a compilation of any author's works; for a while thereafter it was prohibited to read any book titled "complete works." Other volumes in the same format or from the same publisher that were also called *Complete Works*—by Shakespeare or Oscar Wilde, for instance—were confiscated because of their title and the fact that their physical appearance was similar. Another book that was confiscated was *Cubism*, because the officers believed it was about Cuba, and also one titled *Revolution in Physics*, because of the word "revolution."

One book that was always held up at checkpoints and confiscated was *Mister President*, by Guatemalan Nobel Prize author Miguel Ángel Asturias. Once they figured out that it wasn't related to the Chilean situation, they would pass it through, and then it would again be held up at the next checkpoint.

The only book that I brought with me was *Crime and Punishment* by Dostoyevsky, in French, whose protagonist is named Raskolnikov. A noncommissioned officer came into our barracks to inspect and he picked up the book. He leafed through it but he couldn't read French. What he could decipher was the name Raskolnikov. "Oh, those Russians," he said, disgusted. "Another Communist book!" and he threw it onto the bed.

The radio was a primary source of information. In the first phase we were allowed to listen to a local station that broadcasted the official newscast in the afternoons and evenings. Half the program was dedicated to "proving" that the "Marxists," especially those in the leadership "hierarchy," had been arrested with thousands of escudos,[34] and others with thousands of dollars, still others with weapons. The broadcast called all of us "delinquents."

34. Escudos were the Chilean currency at the time.

Later we received a tiny shortwave radio, even though they were prohibited. At night, around nine or ten o'clock, when the barracks was locked and no one came in to inspect, we would painstakingly find a working station; we called this task "working the waves." Fernando Flores was the expert at this. He realized that by connecting the radio to the stovepipe that went up to the ceiling of the barracks, we could improvise an antenna. In this way we were able to listen to foreign radio stations that provided us with valuable information.

Reading also kept us in good spirits. In the first phase we had novels and some books about experiences that were similar to what we were going through, and we were able to relive and remember the struggle of so many others in similar conditions. We understood that suffering in these circumstances is not an isolated event; rather, it has always been a part of history.

Others read the Bible, which circulated among the prisoners. Passages from the Old and New Testaments were read and discussed with interest and provided relief.

In terms of writing, the rules were much stricter. It took us a long time to obtain blank pages. We began to organize classes to keep our minds occupied with new ideas and tools, and through our delegate those of us studying foreign languages were able to obtain some paper. Each of us got one sheet of paper that had to be in plain sight, together with our pencils, so that it could be inspected at any moment. After a couple of months, we earned the privilege of receiving a notebook. It was an unforgettable ceremony: each notebook had to have its owner's name on it and the pages had to be numbered, so that if necessary we could show what we had written, page by page. Because of the pagination there was no possibility of tearing out a page and writing something different: we were only permitted to write what had already been authorized.

Owning a pencil was an enormous privilege. As in all economies of scarcity, people who had paper and pencils were the most privileged, and their possession constituted a sort of status symbol. For example, it was well known that the delegate and those closest to him had pencils. Others who were very organized held on to their pencil and took good care of it. Pencils could be lent to others, but at some point they began to get lost. Sometimes, if you weren't careful, your pencil could disappear into someone else's hands.

Having food was similar: if someone had a piece of cheese, a jar of condensed milk, a box of cookies, or a piece of chocolate—all scarce goods—everyone would organize around him to share it. Despite the very little that we had, this solidarity continued throughout our imprisonment.

Another important activity was the seminars we organized. After talking with the commander, we were able to structure a program with one or two sessions each week. I was in charge of organizing the sessions, which meant assigning each prisoner a time to present a topic of his expertise. The sessions took place on the days that we didn't have forced labor, due to inclement weather or a change of schedule imposed by the camp commander.

Because of the cold, the sessions took place in the same room so we could be near the stove; we brought some chairs from the "mess hall" tent. The forty-five-minute sessions started at 5:00 p.m., before dinner, followed by thirty minutes of questions. The sessions covered many topics. For instance, Edgardo Enríquez[35] gave an interesting talk about the brain. He was writing a book about brain functioning, and he had written about and researched the topic. The two doctors, Jirón and Guijón, gave a presentation on the evolution of medicine in recent years and trends in the field. Fernando Flores talked about cybernetics. The commander came to his session; after it was over, one of the officers, not to be left out, pointed out that he was aware that computers were being used for accounting and for keeping inventory of weapons and other military supplies. In his mind this made him an expert in computing!

Clodomiro Almeyda gave a talk about the theory of social change. He needed to talk about Marx, but because in all of our sessions there was always someone from the marines supervising us, he referred to him as "the afore-mentioned bearded one." "The aforementioned bearded one" became a topic of conversation in many subsequent sessions! Sergio Vuskovic gave a talk about language and other means of communication in the early stages of man, a topic that he had researched for his thesis before becoming a professor of philosophy.

Jorge Tapia gave a conference about constitutional law. Orlando Letelier spoke about international finances. José Tohá gave a presentation about linguistics and the modern use of Spanish, and he reprimanded us all for our poor use of the language in the camp, inspiring us to use our time there to enrich our vocabularies, grammar, and public speaking abilities.

After the first sessions, the officers stopped attending and started to send noncommissioned officers. I remember that one sergeant approached the doctors after their talk to respectfully ask them to prescribe some medications for his sick wife. Shortly thereafter, the authorities ordered our seminars to end.

We needed activities that would take up time and require a routine: a systemic effort to fill the free time that we had, including Saturdays

35. Edgardo Enríquez was minister of education in the Allende government, and had also been president of the Universidad de Concepción.

and Sundays, so that our minds wouldn't wander or fixate on the circumstances we were subjected to.

In addition to participating in these conversations, we also formed a group to study German. They called us the "Germanophiles." Guijón led it, and Almeyda and I participated, since we had studied German before. At first our only resources were a piece of paper and a pencil. We started by consulting Guijón on this or that word, the most basic vocabulary. Later we obtained some texts and grammar books from Santiago and we started working on reading comprehension.

Looking back, it's amazing to me that we were able to concentrate and to maintain this passion for learning and occupying our minds up until the end. For instance, we were so dedicated to studying German that we tried to have all our conversations in German, even during our forced labor. Later we would even speak German at meals, and we proposed the creation of a "German table." That was where our efforts ended, though, because sitting at a table in a concentration camp speaking German while surrounded by armed officers seemed too similar to a Nazi concentration camp. A few days later, our friends made us shut up and formally asked us to stop speaking German, as they were fed up. So instead we had to isolate ourselves to keep practicing when we were alone.

Finally, we started to teach French. In this case it was my turn to give lessons to the group. My most enthusiastic student was Luis "Lucho" Corvalán,[36] who would later keep several books in French in his bunk bed to translate at night.

Another outlet for us was stone carving. Originally the prisoners from Punta Arenas came up with this craft. Several of us got the idea straight from the noncommissioned officers. One time when we were on the beach, we saw Sergeant Canales—who, like many other noncommissioned officers, behaved well with us—looking for rocks along the water's edge. It was a pebble beach with relatively smooth and soft black stones that were shiny from the tides. With a little piece of wire or a nail file, we would carve little figures in them and trace over the marks incising the stones. Word got out and pretty soon we were all carving stones. It was beautiful to see how everyone wanted to have one, to carve their wives' initials, or their children's, and to keep them close to be given to their loved ones later.

36. Luis Corvalán was a senator and a secretary-general (head) of the Chilean Communist Party.

When we would pass the beaches on our way to work, we would stop to look for stones, carefully choosing one that was the right size or shape to carve our designs. We would choose twenty or thirty at a time. Some people would put them in a bag or jar and would later select the smoothest, softest, nicest ones. We became so involved in this task that we started to collect them. From letters we moved on to animal figures, birds—especially the geese that were so abundant around the island—and sometimes swallows. Some people even carved flowers and landscapes. The prisoners from Punta Arenas did the best designs, and they were able to send them to their loved ones. On a couple of occasions we were able to send some to our families as well, through the Red Cross.

Music also helped lift our spirits. Orlando Letelier was able to have a guitar sent from Punta Arenas, and he would accompany us on cold evenings as we sang around the fire. At around five or six in the afternoon, in the time between returning from work and having dinner, we would set up a bonfire on the patio. It was too crowded in the barracks, and we needed fresh air. We had a half hour to kill so we would sit on benches and sing sentimental songs to raise our spirits. I know that we will always remember Letelier's songs: his boleros, tangos, and Mexican songs.[37]

After Schnake and Lazo left and after the arrival of seven new prisoners, two new groups arrived at Dawson. The first group arrived at the end of November, made up of Luis Corvalán, Anselmo Sule, Pedro Felipe Ramírez, Julio Stuardo, and Camilo Salvo.[38] They arrived at night. Rumors had spread that more people were coming from Santiago, and we were eager to know who they were.

But the officers made us go into our barracks so that we wouldn't see the new prisoners. They brought them into a room adjoining ours, separated only

37. In September 1976 Orlando Letelier was assassinated in Washington, DC, by a car bomb placed and detonated by Michael Townley, an agent of the DINA, Pinochet's secret police. In 1995 DINA chief General Manuel Contreras was convicted of ordering Letelier's assassination and sentenced to life in prison without parole.

38. Anselmo Sule and Camilo Salvo were congressional deputies for the Radical Party. Pedro Felipe Ramírez had been minister of mining and minister of housing for Allende, while Julio Stuardo had been Intendente of Santiago, the capital's appointed governor.

by a partition, so we could hear through it, and we pressed our ears up against the wall to try to recognize any of the voices.

The commander came in and started to give them the same instructions that we had received before: they were prisoners of war; they could not approach the guards nor be within three feet of the barbed wire; if they didn't obey they would be sent to solitary confinement or executed. We listened as the prisoners asked questions—Could they talk? Whom could they talk to? Could they eat?—and we recognized some voices. We were so happy to know that our friends were here because we hadn't heard anything about their whereabouts, only that they had been detained. Despite the material conditions that we found ourselves in, being together meant a lot to them and helped them recuperate from the suffering they had gone through before arriving.

A while later—on the twelfth or thirteenth of December, we were listening to the radio before dinner when we heard that Budnevich and Guijón would be set free. Budnevich was in his room, and Guijón was outside, chopping wood. The news spread fast and filled us with a great sense of joy. We embraced happily. We thought this was the first sign that our confinement would also be ending and we would be coming out of the worst of it. Under those circumstances, when a *compañero* was liberated it was as if we were all set free.

The authorities on Dawson also heard the news by radio, just like us. We asked them how they would implement this decision, and they answered that only when they received the official information by written order would they start the proceedings. Hearing that they would be able to go home was as if we were all going to have the same chance. We never thought, "Why him and not me?" We went to the tent to eat together—anticipating that it would be the last supper there for Guijón and Budnevich. These expressions of solidarity were critical to our well-being.

A few hours after Guijón and Budnevich left the next day, a truck arrived with new prisoners. It was extremely disheartening to see Edgardo Enríquez and Julio Palestro return to Dawson after they had been discharged from the hospitals in Santiago and Punta Arenas, respectively.

Orlando Cantuarias[39] was with them. He had recently left the Swiss embassy and turned himself over to a military patrol car. Cantuarias was motivated by a desire to be with his family. He hadn't been summoned over the radio to

39. Orlando Cantuarias, a leader of the Radical Party, a moderate member of Allende's Popular Unity coalition, had been a minister of mining in his government.

turn himself in, nor was there any charge against him, but his impetuous personality led him to take this step and to present himself to the authorities. He was detained without a trial, despite the fact that on the radio they announced that there were no charges against him and that he might be set free. He was taken to Dawson Island in December 1973. After a while with us, Cantuarias came up with the ironic "Prayer of the Dawson Prisoner":

> God in His infinite goodness
> Knows what is best for us
> We're all screwed here
> His will be done![40]

The saddest thing was the state in which Edgardo Enríquez returned to Dawson. He had been taken to Santiago because of a weak heart, worsened by the labor he was subjected to, the cold, his advanced age (sixty-five years old), and, more than anything, by the pain of his sons' fate.[41] He had first gone to a hospital at Punta Arenas and then to another in Santiago, where he underwent intense treatments. Despite the gravity of his physical situation, he was sent back to Dawson, even though everyone knew that on the island there would be no way to save him in case of an emergency.

When he arrived he was deeply upset: he believed that he might die at any moment. I believe—and he later recognized as well—that the support and company that we provided aided his recovery. His will to survive was very strong.

However, he lived in fear that at any moment he would receive news that one of his sons had died. He had told Dr. Jirón that if this ever happened, he wanted to be told directly, because he intentionally did not read the newspapers or listen to the radio to avoid being confronted by this news. He would receive the dreaded news months later, while under house arrest.

40. Oración del Dawsoniano: "Dios en su infinita bondad / sabe lo que nos conviene / harto jodido nos tiene / ¡hágase Su voluntad!"

41. Miguel and Edgardo, founders and leaders of the Movimiento de Izquierda Revolucionaria (MIR), an extreme group to the left of the Popular Unity, chose to resist the dictatorship with armed struggle. Miguel Enríquez, the charismatic head of the MIR, was killed in a shootout in October 1974. His brother, Edgardo, who replaced him, was disappeared in Buenos Aires in April 1976, shortly after the military coup in Argentina. Their father knew that they were unlikely to survive.

In December—our last month at Compingim—there were some changes in our work assignments. While one squad was tasked with erecting posts, which was now considered relatively easy work, the youngest of us were sent to work on the sewage system near Puerto Harris.

Puerto Harris is a small village that has its charms. We could admire the landscape, the open space, the ocean, the birds, the clouds. The island has a great natural beauty, and Puerto Harris does, too. It's made up of a group of very old houses from the estate that owned it until 1972, an old church, and some new constructions built by naval personnel during the Unidad Popular government.

Our assignment in this town was to replace some small pipes with larger ones so that a greater amount of water could flow. To carry this out, we had to work in clay ditches a meter and a half underground. Because the pipes were often broken, and there was a lot of rain, we were often covered in mud. Some of us had boots, and others worked in their street shoes. We were up to our knees excavating the mud with shovels for hours. This assignment lasted a long time and was one of the toughest on the island during our first months there.

But we also had some lighter and nicer tasks to do in Puerto Harris, such as working on the church. We suggested to Chaplain Cancino that we renovate that small place of worship. Miguel Lawner was a gifted architect. He designed the project and suggested a series of changes. The chaplain got the materials, and we painted the ceilings, doors, and interior, restoring its authenticity. The project was progressing well, but unfortunately the military ordered its suspension.

During the time that we were working in Puerto Harris, we weren't permitted to cross through town, and when we were transported in the dump trucks, we had to crouch down and take a roundabout way so we wouldn't pass the homes or the school where the children were. We were strictly forbidden from being seen or seeing anyone. Being treated like pariahs provoked both sadness and anger in me.

Several accidents occurred on these jobs. The most serious was when Vladimir Arellano and another prisoner had to bring a heavy post and entrench it in the hole we had dug. With any wrong move, it was possible to dislocate a finger, primarily the thumb, or sustain a shoulder injury. Arellano made one slight error in the angle, and all of a sudden he fell to the ground suffering horrible neck pain. He's a very self-controlled and strong man, but we could see on his face that he was really hurt. He started writhing on the ground. It was extremely cold out and he was freezing. I took off my jacket to cover him. We were on a cold plain and there was a chilling wind. An armed corporal supervised the area. When he saw that I had covered Arellano with my jacket, the corporal reprimanded me.

The pain was so strong that Arellano started to lose consciousness. We were far from town and had no medical resources. We implored the corporal to bring Arellano to see Dr. Jirón, but he didn't believe us. We insisted that he go find a vehicle, pointing out that if Arellano died, it would be under his watch. He said there were no vehicles and that we would have to wait another hour or two until one arrived. But we could see in the distance, in Puerto Harris, a blue truck that belonged to the construction firm in charge of the site that we were working on. We all went with the corporal to borrow the truck. When Arellano regained consciousness the pain was so strong that he couldn't hold back the tears and tremors. When he arrived at the camp, they could only give him a tranquilizer.

The next day he was transferred to the hospital in Punta Arenas, where they took an X-ray and confirmed that his elbow was broken and there was a trapped nerve. He was operated on and spent four months in the hospital in Punta Arenas undergoing physical therapy.

The attitude of the military differed according to their rank: the officers, the noncommissioned officers, and the troops.

Normally the harshest and most drastic orders came from the officers. It's hard to say whether they were so tough with us of their own volition or whether orders to treat us poorly came down from their superiors. However, I could also make a distinction among them, because not all of them behaved similarly. Some maintained a neutral stance, trying to distance themselves from their duty as prison wardens. Others even confessed to us that they were unhappy at being assigned this mission.

The NCOs generally showed more neutrality. Sometimes they acted as shock absorbers between the orders they were given by their superiors and the treatment we actually received, to lessen the violence. We were able to resolve many problems with them, especially if they had any autonomy or if the instructions that they received were not very precise so that they wouldn't be disciplined in retaliation. There was no hate, no ideological scheme that made them think that we had set out to "destroy our nation." On the contrary, oftentimes they would recognize just who we political prisoners were, and after a few days a more humane relationship would be established.

There was a different attitude altogether among the troops. Many of them came from the central region of Chile and from urban areas (Santiago, Valparaíso, Concepción). They were from the working class and therefore had a greater sensitivity. Many of them told us that they were under great pressure from their superiors, who had told them not to establish contact with the prisoners or they would be punished. When conditions allowed—especially when we went out into the field—the relationships changed. Sometimes they expressed disagreement with the military government. They talked about how they had to act against other recruits who had refused to repress their own people, during the first days of the coup. Others told us how they had friends who were their own parents' jailers. More than one confided that their brothers were detained and that their families were starving.

We also felt a change as the months went by. Little by little we noticed how an attitude of hate was being inculcated in many officers, NCOs, and troops, and in the conscripts doing their military service.

Attitudes were at their most flexible during the beginning of our imprisonment. In order to avoid empathy, they took new measures so that a team of officers, NCOs, or troops would never stay with us for more than two weeks. Later we noticed that the troops were harangued when they arrived; more than once we heard them being addressed and told that they should be very careful around us because we were delinquents who at any moment might attempt to disarm them.

Shortly after the coup, the junta claimed to have discovered the existence of a "Plan Zeta" ("Plan Z"), whose alleged objective was to assassinate people in the opposition, to oust the higher-ups in the armed forces, and to eliminate political and even business leaders. The troops were told that because of Plan Z, we intended to kill them all. At one point posters were put up in cafeterias and shops in the areas where soldiers lived, with photos of a soldier with a superimposed Z, indicating that he was a target of "Plan Z."[42]

This fear of us as "delinquents" was clear in the case of the first chaplain. A few days after we arrived on the island, some of us asked that a chaplain be brought in. Cancino arrived a few weeks later. He was young, about thirty years old. At first he seemed a bit fearful of us. He confided later that when he had first arrived, he was afraid to enter the camp. Little by little as he began to get to know the prisoners, the fear melted away. He realized the injustices that had been done to us. He understood the pain of being taken away from our families, with relatives and friends who were killed with no defense. We forged a real connection with him, and after a while we asked him if he could call our families when he was in Punta Arenas to let them know that we were alright and to ask them to send a few things.

---

42. For a critical analysis of this fabricated "Plan Z," see Steve J. Stern, *Battling for Hearts and Minds: Memory Struggles in Pinochet's Chile, 1973–1988* (Durham, NC: Duke University Press).

Considering that we were supposedly a group of belligerent and aggressive prisoners, one can understand why the concentration camp would be scary to some people. The priest had told us that he had heard terrible things about us before he arrived, and that at first he had been afraid that we would take him hostage and use him as leverage for negotiation. But we had a good relationship with the chaplain, and the chance to express our problems, thoughts, and feelings was a great relief even if it couldn't change our situation. We asked if he would serve as an intermediary with the camp authorities, to make life a bit easier. It was with him that we came up with the idea of renovating the little church.

Unfortunately, after a while the chaplain's luck shifted. One day he went to Punta Arenas and apparently told the other clergymen about his experience at Dawson—they were intrigued to hear about it—and this information may have reached others as well. When he got back to the island, the house that he lived in with the priests had been searched, and some colleagues were afraid of being detained. The chaplain left again and never came back, though we asked about him repeatedly. We later learned that his post had been terminated and another chaplain replaced him. We were told that this new chaplain was at Baker and other islands. When we requested that he come to Dawson, we were told he was too busy. In the end we understood that no chaplain would be allowed to come to Dawson again.

Much later, my wife told me that the chaplain had in fact called our houses as we had requested. In my case, he called her at 1:00 a.m., saying: "Ma'am, this is the Dawson Island chaplain. I'm calling from Punta Arenas on behalf of your husband."

The connection was bad and he sounded very far away. Given the time and the fact that a chaplain was calling, my wife feared the worst.

"What happened to my husband?" she asked.

"Nothing, don't worry," he replied. "Your husband is fine, but he wants you to send him some books so that he can study German."

After the chaplain left, we held our own religious services led by the prisoners on Sunday mornings, and we read passages from the Bible.

Even though measures were taken to harden the attitudes of those in uniform toward us, the relationship between the soldiers and the prisoners was also sometimes relaxed. For example, although we were prohibited from coming within ten feet of them, several times we played soccer games, us against the soldiers, on a gravel field surrounded by barbed wire fences. They also asked us if we would make designs on the black stones for them to bring home as a souvenir. Later the soldiers themselves started to do small favors for us, such as bringing packages to the city to be sent to our families. This was true of the personnel from both the navy and the army, because around that time members of the latter arrived to serve in rotation with the marines.

One time, a group of soldiers came into the room at night and started to walk through, bunk by bunk. I didn't know what it was about until they got to my bed. They were armed and we were afraid. We got a big surprise when we learned that what they wanted from us was to get our autographs, so that they could have them as souvenirs. They wanted to prove to their parents that we were indeed the people they were guarding.

During this last phase in Compingim, through December 1973, there were some friendly relationships between the military and the prisoners. Later we learned that this caused a reaction in the army. Some troops were suspended, and those that they could prove had been in direct contact with us—because they carried carved black stones, money, or other things for the families of political prisoners—were sent to solitary confinement. From then on conditions worsened and they kept their distance from us. The biggest concern of the officers was to prevent contact between the troops and the political prisoners.

But we could observe different behaviors among soldiers and sailors. There was a noncommissioned officer who arrived in November or December who seemed affable. He decided that we should pray at night, since he was used to praying and thanking God for everything that he had received. Some people who had a stronger connection with the Catholic Church didn't like the fact that other people without religious beliefs would be forced to pray. So one night a group of us told him that many prisoners weren't Catholic but they shared humanist and Christian beliefs, and it would be better not to force them to pray. We asked if instead we could read something out loud from the Bible. He agreed, and so one night he had us line up outside, in the cold, and he gave us a few minutes to "meditate," as he called it. Fernando Flores and I chose a passage that night from the Sermon on the Mount, powerful pages from the Bible validating the persecuted, the imprisoned, and the suffering. The following night the Bible reading was suspended and that was the end of the experience.

This particular noncommissioned officer was known for his paternal tone. At the end of each day, when we were already in our beds, he would come in to say goodnight and give us tips about how to withstand our situation.

The friendships and connections formed under these types of circumstances are very solid, especially when a group of people fears death. When there are no material goods to show off to others, we see each person stripped naked, with all his virtues and weaknesses. In these situations, people really get to know one other. To experience shared pain is a communion with a powerful and binding tie. The strength with which we were able to bear our circumstances was possible because of the solidarity, human warmth, and efforts of each of us to lift the others' spirits. During that time we had innumerable occasions to talk and get to know each other. Together every minute of every day, our personalities were on display.

I remember the entertaining case of Julio Palestro. He was funny. We would be crowded into the barracks, looking for ways to distract ourselves, and Julio would take over the "auditorium," describing his culinary experiences to us. His voice was low and smooth—he was in a very weak physical state—and he would start by saying, "What are we going to eat today?" And he would continue, "Well, today we're going to eat . . ." And he would describe the menu: the appetizer, how it would be prepared, what condiments he would add, at what temperature it would be cooked. "Well, Julio, and the main course?" And he would describe it. Then the dessert, and how it would be served. He went on: "Well, with the first course I'm going to serve a red wine . . ." And he would specify the vineyard and year. He had an amazing wealth of culinary knowledge. We would be laughing like crazy listening to him. Even in these conditions, eating only beans and feeling constant hunger pangs, we found ways to create good humor.

Adolfo Silva was another fellow prisoner, known for always being in a bad mood. He rarely took his cigarette out of his mouth, he groaned all the time, and he liked to call out the others. But he had a strong will. Silva had back problems and had to stay in the camp. One of his jobs was to wash our work clothes. In the morning he would get a bin full of water and some tree bark and other plants and he would wash all our clothes—socks, underwear, shirts, handkerchiefs—and he would hang them on the barbed wire to dry. When we came back from work, we would see the clothes hanging up on the wire so that we could wear them the following day, since we didn't have many clothes at that time.

Later, "old Silva" took care of the shower, which was heated by a kind of wood-burning stove that had to be regulated so that the water would be at a good temperature. There was a drum with a floater—just a little medicine bottle—that allowed him to check if the water was high or not. He did all this work willingly, but always moaning and groaning, and he became famous for this attitude. He was so obsessed with cigarettes that at night, when smoking was strictly forbidden, Silva would light a cigarette butt under the blanket and exhale by giant mouthfuls, making him vulnerable to severe punishment.

Aniceto Rodríguez was very meticulous, and obsessed with cleanliness and orderliness, and was a bit grumpy about it. But this was nonetheless an attractive personality trait.

Enrique Kirberg, also known for orderliness, went to the extreme—he always made sure that his watch had exactly the right time, whereas many of the rest of us didn't even know what day it was. He made sure that it coincided exactly with the whistles at 12:00 p.m. and 3:00 p.m. He made a calendar to know exactly what day it was. From my bunk next to his, I could see his calendar. One morning I stayed in bed because I could see that on his calendar it said "Holiday." But I was shaken by the order to get up and line up for work right away. I was annoyed and I asked Kirberg what was going on. He said it wasn't actually a holiday: he had made his own calendar and that day corresponded to his birthday.

He had a special piece of wood at the foot of his bunk bed like a doormat, so that everything would be clean. He also made a special hanger out of wire and a rod to hang everything, including the shirt that he washed daily.

Edgardo Enríquez was always impeccable; every detail of his life reflected an admirable dignity. He always wore a white shirt and a tie, which he also washed every day. His shoes were always polished. He was always in good spirits, strong as a rock and improving everyone else's mood.

There's an anecdote about his tie that's very telling. We were in the worst circumstances and we didn't even have time to wash our clothes: most of us wore one pair of blue jeans for three or four weeks, but Don Edgardo never abandoned his white button-up shirt and tie. One day one of us asked him: "Listen, Don Edgardo, why do you wear a tie every day? Doesn't it bother you?"

Don Edgardo looked at him and answered in his characteristic tone: "Look, my friend: to be frank, of everything that we are going through here, the tie is what bothers me the least."

Daniel Vergara told me a very nice anecdote about Edgardo Enríquez. When they were both in the hospital in Punta Arenas, Don Edgardo had told him about a classmate of his from Concepción, named Otárola: "At the Universidad de Concepción when I was a student, there was a guy named Otárola. Otárola was a very distinguished student and he got the best grades. Otárola was the most popular. Otárola was at the top, a brilliant guy." And he continued, reciting all of Otárola's virtues, and he finished by saying, "But Otárola was in second place, because I was in first."

Clodomiro Almeyda was another character. He wasn't very coordinated with his hands, so he had to be helped to do a lot of things. But he never shirked from any physical task: he carried posts and dug holes with a shovel and a stick but always a bit clumsily. He had the ability to stay calm and disconnected from the conditions of a life that depressed a lot of us. There was a wisdom to his personal style, and we couldn't tell whether he really noticed his surroundings. He was also very distracted, which provoked a lot of laughter and made him the butt of many harmless jokes.

There was one morning when—as usual—we had just a few minutes to bathe in the stream before getting back in line. At that moment Cloro—as we called him—started going around asking nervously, "Has anyone seen my toothbrush?" We broke into laughter: "Cloro," I told him, "it's in your mouth!"

José Tohá knew Cloro from when they were children, and he had innumerable anecdotes that he amused us with. When we would go into the field to work, at lunchtime we would huddle up wherever the wind was weakest; we would make a fire, and after eating our beans, we would sit and talk. José would spend the time telling jokes, and he would tell us stories about Clodomiro that showed the extent of his distraction. One story related what had happened on a morning that they had a meeting in Belgium with King Balduino when Clodomiro was minister of foreign affairs. Protocol allowed for a fifteen- to twenty-minute meeting. The night before, Cloro had slept very poorly and it appeared that the king had as well. Both of them started to yawn. The king brought Cloro to another room, where they sat in a comfortable sofa facing a window looking out onto the garden. After a while Cloro said, "Well, Your Majesty, if you are tired, we can rest for a few minutes." Both of them fell fast asleep. The meeting went on for twenty-five, thirty, forty minutes. Outside, the journalists covering Almeyda's visit began to speculate: what was so important that King Balduino was still talking with the Chilean foreign representative? They woke up, said two or three things, and went out. "Imagine the little nap that Cloro took with the king!" Tohá told us laughing.

Another tragicomic anecdote happened on a workday during our lunch break. We had a little radio with us, and by chance we were able to capture an Argentine news station. According to the newscaster, because of the allegations against Clodomiro Almeyda he could spend over one hundred years in prison. With sadness and irony, Cloro exclaimed, "But, man, how am I going to live long enough to complete the sentence?!"

Vladimir Arellano was the coffee drinker of the group. Generally we would make a fire outside at night before going to bed, and we would try to get some coffee and sugar. We would heat it up in a can and serve it in sardine tins. We had fewer than eight tins. Then we got some little cans, and each of us made his own "mug" with a handle made of wire.

We also shared a curious experience with Julio Stuardo. The first days that we went out to the forced labor were very rainy ones. One afternoon our squad was lucky enough to be close to the home of a tenant, whose last name was Pérez. He treated us very well. He invited us into his home to shelter us and prepared some onions and lamb meat in a large pan. We shared two or three afternoons with Pérez. Later we learned that he was forced to leave his house and the island.

In his yard there were big empty barrels. The wind would blow from the coast toward the strait, so one day Julio and I started joking that we might be able to escape in one of those barrels. We put a couple into the water to see how they would float. Stuardo took it more seriously, and decided to build a kind of raft. Max Marholz said he was a good sailor and he could steer the rafts. It was an outlandish idea: the cold was battering and the water was freezing; anyone who fell in would not last more than a few minutes and we had no idea in which direction we would steer it. But it was a good distraction. Later we weren't allowed to even approach the barrels.

Miguel Lawner spent many hours drawing landscapes, island scenes, figures, and sketches of us working. During any free moment, he would draw. Many of his drawings were saved and later published, showing a real artistic sense and ability to capture the place, the people, and the natural surroundings.

Sometimes, even though we were prisoners to the island, we were still absorbed by its beauty, by the coast, the pebble beaches, and steppes: a very light-colored meadow, almost yellow, at the edges of the forest. In the areas where there were trees, the wave of green continued almost to the ocean's edge. To perceive the vastness and calm brought us peace. We were dazzled by the beauty of the clouds, their shapes and colors that drew us into a magical world.

There were huge trunks in the middle of the steppes, many of them scorched, revealing the existence of ancient forests, and it was said that some remained in the center of the island. Behind the barracks there was a forest where we got wood to chop for the kitchen and the woodstove. We found ancient cypresses, and we would cut them down with axes and carry them to the kitchen.

From the beach we could watch the Commerson dolphins, the most beautiful dolphins in the Chilean ocean. Often, while we were working near the ocean, we would see groups of four or five just meters from the shore; they would dance and leap out of the water with their whole bodies, dive down, and resurface.

On days when the officers had a touch of humanity, we would go shell fishing on those beaches. We would find mussels and sea urchins, to make up for the lack of food we were given.

There was a spectacular variety of birds. The most typical—the ones we would carve into stones—were the *caiquenes*, a kind of geese typical of southern Chile. They were bigger than ducks and more refined. Their takeoffs were clumsy, but once they were in the air, they flew with amazing speed. They would travel in couples, the male one color, the female another.

Among the special activities of our daily lives on Dawson, on Sundays we took out the mattresses, shook them out, and then put two or three blankets outside in the sun. The mattresses were damp, dirty, and old. At around 10:00 a.m., if it wasn't raining, we would bring everything outside and put it on benches or chairs, or would hang them from the barbed wire fences. The mattresses didn't fit in this little area, so we would rotate every half hour to air everything out. It was a depressing scene—a small patio full of stripped mattresses and dark blankets on the gravel ground, surrounded by barbed wire and lots of prisoners crowded into a corner so that there would be space for the mattresses.

As time passed, we were sent out to install telephone poles at sites that were farther and farther away. The squads that were furthest along in their work began to get closer and closer to a camp that was being built, although we didn't know for what purpose.

The first groups to approach the construction site didn't pay much attention, until we heard that that site was meant for us and for new prisoners who would be arriving on the island. To us, this didn't seem possible, and we accused the rumor spreaders of being pessimists. I have to confess that at the beginning I didn't really pay attention. Later, when we realized that we might really be brought there, a wave of desperation flowed over us. We felt the weight and the impotence of seeing ourselves caught up in something that could last for an important part of our lives, if indeed we were to get out alive. As the new campsite was being completed and closed in with fencing, the sensation only grew in intensity.

Little by little, everything began to take on the feeling of a concentration camp: huge barbed wire fences, small interior spaces, large barracks where up to eighty people would fit. It had never occurred to me that we would be locked up in a camp like this, because in Compingim, although we were enclosed, there was at least a bit more space because those barracks had been built for the troops. Even though they had installed barbed wire fences, there was still a sense of humanity to the place. The distribution of space and construction weren't intended to pile people up and lock them in, like in the new place.

At the same time, though, we received some hopeful signs. Maybe we were desperate to find the inkling or possibility of an exit in any sentence, in any detail. Sometimes we received letters and messages from the people who visited the island; they told us to have faith, that there could be some news soon, to not be disappointed.

José Tohá received a document from the chemistry department of an American university—it was about scientific topics and seemed to be completely unrelated to our situation. He held on to it for three or four days. No one knew what it was about, until one day I picked it up and said: "Wait a minute, maybe there's some kind of message in here." José had said more than once that he had friends in associations all over the world who were striving for peace and for the liberation of people they knew.

We huddled around and held the pages up to the light until we noticed that some letters had little dots over them. I picked up the document and half-jokingly started to dictate the letters with dots on top of them, and after going through the three or four pages we deciphered a message that said, in English, "José, resist. Many people are worried. Ted[43] is doing everything he can." We didn't look into it further, and José later destroyed the letter, but it surprised and encouraged us.

At the beginning of December, we still harbored hopes of being released before Christmas, because of the religious and personal signifi-cance of that date. This rumor had been spreading around, and we even heard that it was a headline in one of the newspapers in Santiago around December 13 or 14: "Amnesty likely for prisoners before Christmas."

We clung to this idea, but nothing happened. We later learned that the amnesty was for common criminals but not for political prisoners.

Our fellow prisoners from Punta Arenas were also in the dark. Sometimes they told us we would be moved to another campsite. For them, the situation was even hazier, because although they were in close proximity to their families, in their home territory and acclimatized, at the same time they were randomly removed and brought to Dawson with some frequency. Generally they came in groups of eight or ten. One would be liberated and four or more would be locked in the dungeons of a regiment ground. Others were beaten and tortured.

43. "Ted" possibly refers to US senator Edward "Ted" Kennedy.

Many of them came back deteriorated and demoralized. Arturo Jirón, as our doctor, was always ready to tend to them, and the camp commander had also ordered him to give them checkups. Because of his singular role, we knew he would not be killed. Many men left with relatively good health and came back destroyed: some were missing teeth, others had burn marks on their backs, some had broken bones or bruises all over their bodies.

Besides being beaten and receiving electric shocks, some told us that they were shut up for several days in metal containers with other prisoners, with no food and no place to take care of their bodily functions. They had bags under their eyes, and they were both psychologically and physically destroyed: they were being primed for interrogation. Some were tied up with ropes and sub-merged into the freezing Straits of Magellan. They would be left there for a while and then taken out, and it went on like this. Others told of how they had to run barefoot over a bed of thorns.

There were cases of strong and healthy people, like Márquez, a peasant leader from the area who was in stupendous physical condition for months with a great serenity and capacity for work. He was taken away and when he was brought back a month later, he was a different man. Although he was only thirty-five years old, he looked like an old person. They had broken his teeth, he had lost thirty pounds, his gaze was glazed over, and he no longer had any capacity to resist.

This was also the case of Aristóteles España, a seventeen-year-old university student leader. He was brutally beaten and mistreated. He began to have nightmares, and we would all know it because his screams could be heard across the barracks. Then his barracks-mates would knock on the partition wall, calling for a doctor, and Guijón or Jirón would go. The only thing they could do was to give him an injection of tranquilizer, because he needed a treatment that was impossible to get on the island.

Tension and fear manifested themselves in different ways. The fear of being brought to trial—which was happening to others—to then be condemned to ten, twenty years in prison, was a sword that hung over us day and night and made things unbearable unless we sought out ways to avoid depression.

One of the prisoners, an economist in charge of the food supply at a school in Punta Arenas, began to suffer from epileptic seizures: he would start to have spasms and fall on the floor and we would have to call a doctor right away. One night someone had a heart attack and there was no way to tend to him or get him to Punta Arenas at that time of night. If the sea wasn't cooperative, no boats could arrive, and if it was too windy, planes couldn't land. We were completely disconnected from the world.

Sergio Bitar and Jorge Tapia entering Escuela Militar on September 13, 1973. Photograph published in a local newspaper.

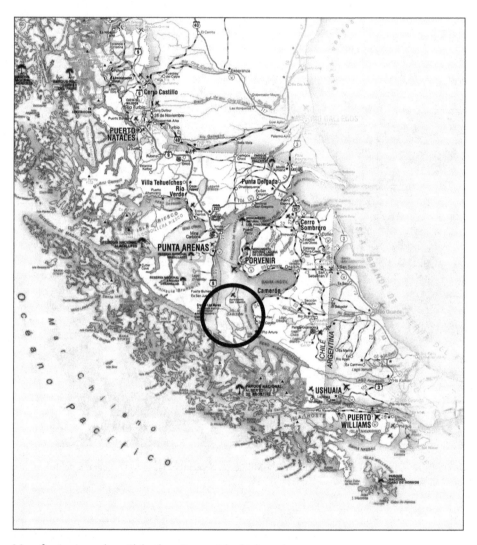

Map of region in southern Chile where Dawson Island is located.

Stgo 28 de D[iciembre]

Mi flaquito querido.

Hoy día retiré en una oficina del Reg[istro]
tu carta del 9 de Diciembre.

[texto censurado]

He quedado algo deprimi-
da por tu carta. Por una parte llegó con
un montón de líneas censuradas (más
que en las anteriores) y por otra, me in-
quieta tu salud (física y anímica). ¿Has
vuelto a tener problemas con tu estómago?
Por favor ¡cuídate! En cuanto al ánimo -
comprendo que flaquee a veces - esto tarda
tanto - pero debes superarlo como sea. Por
nosotros - no te preocupes. Yo estaré firme
mientras sepa que estés bien. así que
por favor no pienses demasiado y trata de
pasar lo mejor de estos duros meses. La
separación es muy dura, pero al mismo
tiempo enseña tanto. Creo que valorare-
mos mucho más nuestra futura vida en
común y nuestra mutua compañía (siem-
pre lo he hecho - creo que aquí tú tienes
más que aprender que yo).

En tu casa mis pequitas si tengo información respecto a la situación de Uds.
Mi vida, ojalá la tuviera. Rumores corren
muchos - pero a esos no les hago caso -
e información oficial no hay ninguna.

Censored letter from Kenny Hirmas de Bitar to Sergio Bitar.

ESTUDIO EN RITOQUE ABRIL '75

Orlando Letelier. Drawing by Miguel Lawner.

Top left: Lieutenant Jaime Weidenlaufer's first speech to the prisoners. Drawing by Miguel Lawner.

Bottom left: Study session at Ritoque. Drawing by Miguel Lawner.

CERTIFICADO.
=============

* SANTIAGO El Jefe de Zona en Estado de Sitio de la Provincia de Santiago que suscribe, certifica que el Sr. SERGIO BITAR CHACRA, se encuentra en libertad bajo registro domiciliario y control de la Autoridad Militar, según lo dispuesto en el Decreto Exento N°443 de 30 de Septiembre de 1974.

Está autorizado para efectuar diligencias fuera de su hogar.

En consecuencia el Sr. BITAR, deberá mantenerse dentro de los límites de la Provincia de Santiago, debiendo requerir la autorización de esta Jefatura, cada vez que deba abandonar la Jurisdicción de esta Zona en Estado de Sitio.

Santiago,01 de Octubre de 1974.-

SERGIO ARELLANO STARK
General de Brigada
Jefe de Zona en Estado de Sitio
Provincia de Santiago.

"TRABAJEMOS POR UN CHILE PROSPERO Y LIBRE"   Form. 501

TELEGRAFO DEL ESTADO (CHILE)

N°.......... Depositado el .... «REALIZAREMOS EL .... Valor 513
                                       MILAGRO CHILENO»
Para cualquier reclamo, sirvase presentar este recibo.

N9   ESP   130 DE SANTIAGO TPH NR   547   26   27   1320

    Fecha .... A .....

    SERGIO   BITAR   ISLA   DAWSON   TERCERA   ZONA   NAVAL

    PUNTA ARENAS =

    FELICES   33 ANOS PUNTO   GIRE   LOS PROXIMO SEAN
    MEJORES PUNTO COFIAMOS VERTE PRONTO BESOS =

    JENNY JAVIER   RODRIGO   PATRICIA

                                              CENSURADO

"TRABAJEMOS POR UN CHILE PROSPERO Y LIBRE"

    DATOS DEL REND. COL   547 + +   53 + + +   TRANSMISION

Nombre ....
Firma ....
Domicilio ....

OBSERVACIONES: El Estado no se responsable por pérdidas, daños o perjuicios ocasionados por errores en transmisión, demoras, malas entregas o faltas de datos o por otros motivos cualesquiera; pero en ciertos casos las tasas percibidas serán reembolsadas en su totalidad o en parte.   Imp. Correos y Telégrafos - C.

Improvisational mug made by a prisoner at Dawson.

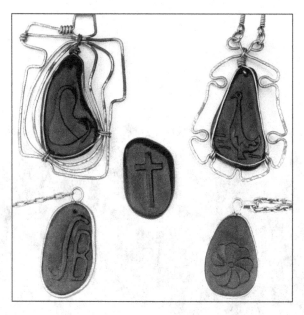

Stones carved by Sergio Bitar.

Top left: Certificate issued following house arrest, granting Sergio Bitar freedom to circulate in Santiago so long as he is under registration.

Bottom left: Telegram from Sergio Bitar's family wishing him a happy thirty-third birthday.

Flag-raising ceremony at Compingim.

Prisoners lined up upon arrival at Dawson. *First row, from left*: Aniceto Rodríguez, Clodomiro Almeyda, Vladimir Arellano, Aníbal Palma, Osvaldo Puccio Jr., Carlos Jorquera, José Tohá, Hernán Soto, Benjamín Teplisky, Enrique Kirberg, Arturo Jirón, Miguel Lawner, Alfredo Joignant, Max Marholz, and Miguel Muñoz. *In the second row*: Tito Palestro, Carlos Matus, and Osvaldo Puccio Sr.

Church at Puerto Harris, rehabilitated by the prisoners at Dawson.

Army barge facing Dawson Island.

Prisoners walking back from work at Dawson: Hernán Soto, Carlos Matus, Benjamín Teplisky, Héctor Olivares, Vladimir Arellano, Miguel Lawner, Carlos Jorquera, Clodomiro Almeyda, and Sergio Bitar. Photograph by Abel Esquivel.

Trucks used for transporting materials and people to worksites.

The wives of political prisoners. *From left*: Kenny Hirmas de Bitar, Cecilia Bachelet de Miranda, Isabel Margarita Morel de Letelier, Hortensia Bussi de Allende, Moy Morales de Tohá, and Angélica Beas de Jorquera.

Río Chico

One day, I think it was December 15, we were told that we had thirty minutes to get our things together: "Get your clothes and blankets and line up outside." We gathered our few things and our "treasures"—a book, a notebook, a can of condensed milk—in a box or some pieces of cardboard and lined up in the courtyard. We waited there all morning, until a dump truck arrived and we put our things inside. Then, like cattle, we all climbed into another truck, surrounded by armed guards and vehicles. We set off to our new site.

The morning of that same day, Carlos Matus had come up to me and nervously told me: "Last night I dreamt that we received orders to pack up our things, line up in the courtyard, and wait, to be taken far from here. I saw it all so clearly: I am sure that today we are leaving Dawson."

Indeed we were leaving the camp, but we weren't going where Carlos had hoped in his dream.

We were going to a real concentration camp.

The new site was tucked in a little hollow next to the coast, a sort of narrow valley surrounded by medium-sized hills. The camp was encircled by a double set of four-meter-high barbed wire fences; the top part of the fence was at an angle similar to the fences in Nazi concentration camps. The dimensions were about 150 by 100 meters. Within this rectangle there were six to eight barracks, long buildings about forty meters long by five meters wide. Everything was built with very light material, wood covered with particleboard on the walls and ceiling protected with zinc planks—hardly appropriate materials for the freezing temperatures.

Inside, bunk beds hung from the beams—forty bunks in the eighty-meter-long room. It was a dark and dismal scene. In the whole structure there were four little windows. In our case, they weren't shielded from the outside; local prisoners from Magallanes told us of iron bars on their windows.

Four or five of the barracks were for prisoners. Others were meant for the kitchen and mess hall, and there were special barracks at the entrance for the troops guarding the camp.

Outside of this fenced-in area there was a road and, across the way, some little houses for the rest of the troops and officers and other enclosures for their cafeteria and dining area.

Each of our barracks inside the fenced quadrangle had another set of barbed wire fences surrounding it, covered in zinc siding so that we wouldn't be seen. Beyond this layer of protection, each barracks had only one entrance, an enormous front door that was closed from the outside with a bar so that at night we were locked in.

In the hills around the camp there were watchtowers, the same kind we had seen in movies and read about in books about concentration camps. There were guards there day and night, with binoculars and machine guns. On top of that, because the island belonged to the navy, there were also nearby bunkers with heavy artillery positioned around the area, supposedly to ward off seaborne attacks. Navy officers worked on the island, but there were also four or five peasants who had been living there before and were now given a deadline by when they had to abandon their farms.

Inside each barracks there were big tin can containers cut in half that acted as washbasins. There were also showers; the water was heated in a pot over the fire. Once or twice a week one of us was permitted to add firewood to keep the water drums full of hot water, such that at 9:00 p.m. those who wanted to could shower in rapid succession. We couldn't use any of those facilities during the day, only a toilet consisting of a hole and two marks indicating where we should stand.

Outside there was a little stone and earth courtyard that we looked after, cleaning and arranging it to avoid the muddy floods that the rains could provoke. There were completely unsanitary latrines in little huts with a hole in the ground and half doors made of zinc. There were only three latrines for thirty-five prisoners.

From that moment on, our prison name Sierra was changed to Isla. I became *Isla 10* (I-10).

Our way of life also changed. We woke up at 6:30 a.m. and had thirty minutes of obligatory exercise before washing ourselves and making our beds. We would tidy up and then have a cup of tea with bread before heading out to work for the day. At night we had to be inside the barracks at 7:30 p.m. When the door was locked from the outside, we were warned that if anyone tried to leave, he would risk being shot. We had to make signs with a white handkerchief and yell so that they would see us. At 10:00 p.m. they turned out the lights. Any reading we had been doing was over.

There was a woodstove in the middle of the big room to keep it warm, an iron cylinder with a pipe to the ceiling. It needed to be stoked with wood throughout the night. At first we organized ourselves into rotating pairs, so that each night two people would stay awake watching over the boiler so that there wouldn't be a fire or the wood wouldn't burn out. The rotating "night watchmen" were also responsible for waking up anyone having nightmares and for looking out for the sick.

There are photos and some footage of this camp. In January, just a few days after arriving, a North American delegation of journalists visited the camp; they were preparing a report for NBC, and they were accompanied by cameramen from the BBC. They had already been in Compingim, which though shocking was nothing compared to this. They filmed inside the camp and from the hills, so there could be a full appreciation of the site. I later learned that the footage was shown in the United States and Europe, including interviews with some of us. My wife told me that some friends who were studying in California at the time called her from the United States to tell her that they had seen me on the television and that I seemed to be in good health.

At one point, some workers were brought to make electrical repairs in one of the barracks. We weren't supposed to speak to them, but we were able to get close enough to have a few words. They told us that a German had helped design the camp. Rumor spread that Walter Rauff[44] was consulting on the project.

We were forced to sing the national anthem twice a day. Under the circumstances, it was painful for us to sing a song that to us represented our country's democratic tradition and our ideals and that now symbolized our imprisonment. It took both consternation and strength to sing this verse out loud:

44. Walter Rauff was one of the most wanted Nazi war criminals to escape to South America after World War II. An SS colonel who invented a way of transforming trucks into mobile gas chambers, Rauff found refuge in Chile, where a 1963 Supreme Court decision protected him from extradition. After the coup, he served as an adviser to the Pinochet dictatorship and was rumored to have helped design its concentration camps, torture chambers, and prisons.

That you be the tomb of the free
or asylum for the oppressed.[45]

But, just like in so many other concentration camps, although we started singing in low voices, we became louder and louder so that it became a real battle cry when two hundred voices echoed the words "or asylum from oppression." More than once, an officer approached us to tell us that we had to sing the entire song at the same volume or we would be punished.

A few months later, they added a new verse for us to sing every morning and night. The verse went:

Your names, brave soldiers
who've been the backbone of Chile
are etched on our chests
so that our children will know them as well.[46]

Throughout our stay at all the camps—Dawson, Puchuncaví, and Ritoque, in my case—we were subjected to attacks and defense simulations about once a week. Apparently they really thought it plausible that Dawson might be attacked by submarines or foreign planes that would come rescue the Popular Unity "hierarchy." This happened especially when marines guarded us. They would pose in different positions and start shooting, aiming toward the coast as if they were warding off an attack. Later they had heavier machine guns and then finally canons that had been moved close to us. There were fifteen, twenty minutes of heavy firing and soldiers running all over the place. The whole thing was deafening.

We had been warned that during the attack simulations we must stay in position wherever we were, because if anyone moved he would be considered a member of the subversive attackers and would be killed immediately. So whenever these maneuverings began, we always stayed motionless.

From the day we arrived at Río Chico, all we ate was lentils in a watery soup; every once in a while we would be given beans. This diet didn't change until May, when we left Dawson and were transferred to the central region of the

45. "Que la tumba serás de los libres / o el asilo contra la opresión."
46. "Vuestros nombres, valientes soldados / que habéis sido de Chile el sostén / nuestros pechos los llevan grabados / lo sabrán nuestros hijos también."

country. The prisoners who had health problems and couldn't digest these foods—diabetics, or people with stomach or liver problems—were very adversely affected.

Sometimes the lentils hadn't even been rinsed and strained: they were mixed with little pebbles, which caused dental problems for many of us. We would arrive to the table starving, and when we started chewing it was impossible to avoid biting into a stone. Lucho Vega and Lucho Corvalán both lost teeth in this way. I broke a molar, as did several others. When this happened, we would go to Luis Belmar, a fellow prisoner from Punta Arenas, who was a dentist. He had very few tools with which to work. His only materials were little nails or pieces of metal and sometimes some dental cement to cover it up. If it were a very serious case, the dentist would inject a painkiller, because there was no hope of any actual treatment. In Vega's case, several months later he had an X-ray that confirmed that his tooth was being held in place by a thumbtack.

Our families continued to make a huge effort to send us food supplies. They knew we had lost weight and that we were subjected to forced labor, with insufficient nutrition. They no longer received our salaries, and many wives and other relatives had been fired from their jobs. So it was a big sacrifice to gather together canned preserves, dried fruit, or chocolate to send to us. The worst of it was that many times what they sent never made it into our hands: in the censored letters we could sometimes read crossed-out words, and they usually said something like: "Here's the list of what I'm sending," followed by all the things they had sent that we never received.

They also censored indications of the amount of money that they sent, because at one point we had the opportunity to buy goods from Punta Arenas. When we first complained about this, they told us that the money they retained would be pooled to create a common fund. However, such funds were never distributed.

I have to confess that it was the first time in my life that I felt real and persistent hunger, and many times I felt dizzy and weak. Having a second piece of bread at dinner became a privilege. When this happened, we would break it into several pieces to share with the others, and keep a portion for the morning coffee.

As time went by, some prisoners forged a good relationship with the cook, who was more permanent than many of the staff. That's how they would get any extra bones that were left over. This operation became almost routine. At around eleven in the morning, the prisoners who were not out in the field would take a plate to the kitchen to ask for five or six bones with a bit of meat on them. They would shave each bone with a knife, add some salt, and give a little to everyone.

At around the same time, we asked permission to harvest the tiny mussels from the shore when we were working nearby. We would make a little bonfire and put them in a can to cook, and we would eat them right there on the beach. We would also get *calafates*, a little plant with little tiny red fruits, like a blackberry, which could be harvested in January or February. These were the only fresh foods we ate.

During their visits, the International Red Cross recognized this situation. They began sending milk, but it didn't make it to our hands. They also sent canned meat, cookies, and chocolates, which we did receive in minimal quantities.

The Red Cross came again at one of the toughest moments. The officers and visitors discussed our diet, and the officers told them that at the camp the prisoners received the same food as the troops. We knew this wasn't true, because some of our prison mates from Punta Arenas worked as kitchen helpers and saw what each group ate. During the visit, the Red Cross workers inspected the kitchen to see what was being prepared. Then they ate with us. They were served lentils, which was completely different from what they had seen being cooked that morning.

During this time, I became obsessed with vitamin deficiencies, to the point that I sometimes did absurd things. One afternoon when I returned to the barracks after work, Jaime Tohá and Osvaldo Puccio Jr. said to me: "Didn't you get your milk?"

"What milk?" I asked.

"They just gave each of us a packet of dried milk. Go ask them for yours."

I went out through the courtyard and crossed the fence to the kitchen entrance, which was an unusual thing for us to do and could have warranted punishment. The first soldier I asked said that he had no idea what I was talking about. I asked permission to go inside. Inside, I said to the officer in charge, "Good afternoon. I came to get my packet of milk."

He looked at me strangely and said he had no idea what I was talking about and sent me back to the barracks.

When I got back, my friends burst out laughing. Tohá and Puccio had known about my weakness for vitamins and played a practical joke on me. My gullibility had done the rest.

Throughout the rest of December up until New Year's, our work was more circumscribed. We couldn't go around the island, which made us feel claustrophobic. During this time, we kept expecting that something would happen. We were still a few days away from Christmas, and we were anxious to receive news that some of us would be freed. But nothing of the sort happened, and Christmas and New Year's came and went with us still on the island.

Around that time, an army officer named Paris arrived. He ordered us to organize a Christmas party. Many of the prisoners said that they preferred to go to sleep early and forget about everything. Others thought that we should help each other keep our spirits up. Thanks to some special care packages that our wives sent, we put together a little "cocktail" party in the courtyard. We laid out the table with some Christmas breads that we had received from our wives and some jars of preserves from Punta Arenas that good friends of Carlos Morales and Aniceto Rodríguez had courageously dared to send us.

I can clearly remember those scenes: the contrast between the caring and solidarity that grew among us and the conditions we lived in. Next to the barracks, we lay down some planks of wood and set out the food on top. Zinc plates on the barbed wire fences blocked the view, and we were surrounded by armed soldiers. But it was a comforting moment, and we felt a sense of abundance. We even received fresh fruit.

New Year's was different, and we decided to organize a little show in one of the barracks. Alfredo Joignant acted as master of ceremonies, dressed in a funny way, and started to announce the various acts on the program. We had prepared some folk songs to sing with Orlando Letelier on the guitar. Each stanza was dedicated to a fellow prisoner and his most entertaining anecdote. Cantuarias's stanza alluded to how he had left the Swedish embassy to instead come to Dawson. Jorge Tapia performed magic with an egg and finished by breaking it on his assistant's head. Ariel Tacchi sang, dressed up as a chinaman, and told jokes. Enrique Kirberg and Puccio Jr. recited: Enrique hid behind "Puccito" and moved his hands while Puccito recited, and Carlos Morales, an astute English learner, did "simultaneous translation." Looking back it might seem a bit ridiculous, but in that moment, the happy scene helped distract us and lift our spirits.

Something strange happened next. After it struck midnight and we were all hugging and giving each other well wishes for the coming year, a big group of soldiers from the army approached us. They entered the barracks by the back door and circulated among us wishing us a happy new year and telling us softly, "*Compañeros*, be strong because you are not alone. We hope the future won't be as difficult as the present: hold on."

This gesture was very emotional. They told us that many others had wanted to come with them but that they hadn't dared approach us. Later we learned that they were punished, and we could tell that from the treatment given to us by the soldiers who relieved them. A rumor circulated that several dozens of the soldiers who guarded us, belonging to different units, had been sent to the military prison in Santiago and were punished for the deferential treatment they showed the prisoners.

Captain Paris spoke to us on New Year's Day. Nervously, he stood at the front and gave a solemn speech, emphasizing that he hoped that this new year would be better and that our lives would return to normalcy. He said he hoped that this situation would be short-lived and that we could soon rebuild our nation together, because we were all Chileans.

There were also attitudes in stark contrast to this one. For instance, when we wanted to send things back to Santiago, we were told that nothing that we had with us could be returned. In the case of books, they told us: "Once you have finished reading them you can burn them, throw them away, or keep them if you want."

But they could not leave the island.

José Tohá and Osvaldo Puccio Sr. returned to the island the first week of January, after spending ten days in the hospital. We began to see what dangerously poor health Tohá was in, though a more appropriate diet during his stay in Punta Arenas had helped him get a bit better and gain some weight. He suffered metabolic deficiencies and couldn't digest the food we were served on Dawson. Every day he wasted away more.

Around that time, the second round of interrogations began, and they were long and harsh. A man named Figueroa came to Dawson around the tenth or fifteenth of January. He was short and squat and dressed in civilian clothes, and he appeared to be sent by the tax-collecting agency. He was a lawyer and, by coincidence, he had been a classmate of Clodomiro Almeyda at the Universidad de Chile.

He indicated that he had been sent by the Consejo de Defensa del Estado (National Defense Council), which was in charge of defending government properties and other assets. He was very arrogant despite the fact that he knew many of the prisoners personally, having served in the previous administration and having been a classmate or acquaintance of several others. He began the first formal interrogations regarding tax issues.

Each of us was summoned from the barracks, isolated for a few hours, and then brought before this man for the interrogation. Afterward, the interrogated prisoner would be taken to the smallest barracks, where the infirmary was, so that he couldn't communicate with the other prisoners who had yet to be interrogated.

We had been told that the objective of these interrogations was to clarify some matters, and that according to the results they would decide if the prisoner would be freed. In my own case and in general, the questions were all asked in the same hostile tone: "Sir, we are questioning you about your role in the destruction of this country, and in particular, about your assets. Here no one gets away with lying. We have concrete information about what you've done: we have your file here with us. We have investigated everything and we know everything about you, so any lie you tell will be punished."

They continued: "What property do you own? What material things have you purchased since 1968? How did you pay for them? When did you purchase your cars? Your house? How did you pay for it? What else do you have? What other investments are you involved in? What do you mean you don't have anything else?"

After I gave detailed explanations, they started to question me about trips I had taken: "Yes, it seems you've traveled a great deal. In 1970, you traveled to the United States. How did you get to the United States? Then it seems you went to Europe. How did you pay for all of this?"

"Sir, the trip to Europe was funded by the United Nations. And the trip to the United States was to study at Harvard University, with a scholarship financed by the Ford Foundation."

"But then we see that you made two trips to Lima and then were in England."

"Yes, sir, the British government invited me to England."

"And all of these trips, who paid for them?"

All of this revealed a strange obsession with traveling, especially after we compared impressions among the prisoners and noted this pattern.

Then he spoke about other things, gave his opinion about the political situation and about President Allende and the military junta.

Lucho Corvalán told us how Figueroa had said to him: "Look, sir, your life is at stake here, so don't invent falsehoods."

Figueroa returned during the month of August, when we were in Ritoque.

After he had made his interrogations, some soldiers approached us and said, "We've heard that it seems today some of you will be leaving." And indeed, at the beginning of February, José Tohá, Clodomiro Almeyda, Alfredo Joignant, Edgardo Enríquez, and Julio Palestro left for Santiago. It was the last time most of us saw José.

Weeks earlier, we had heard some officers tell Aniceto Rodríguez, "You have half an hour to prepare your things." And then they took him to a boat, a plane, and finally he arrived in Santiago, where he was reunited with his family. Two days after he was released from Dawson, we heard on the radio that he had been freed.

After what happened with Aniceto, we thought that something similar would happen to the rest of us, especially to José Tohá. But for the others, the situation was more doubtful, especially in the case of Joignant, since the campaign against him had been relentless.

In the middle of January, another prisoner arrived: Alejandro Jiliberto, who had been detained in October and subjected to horrible suffering. I don't remember all the details, because in general we tried not to ask questions of people who had been tortured, and instead we sought to foster an environment where they could recuperate with solidarity and camaraderie. However, after a few months passed, we had the chance to talk, and what I remember most about his story are the critical moments of a man on the brink of extreme suffering who sees no exit other than death.

He had been arrested in October 1973. He was tortured by the new intelligence service (Dirección de Inteligencia Nacional, DINA[47]), which sought the addresses of alleged opposition organizers. Then he was brought to Policía de Investigaciones, the Chilean FBI. There he was kept awake for long periods of time. He was continuously mistreated and, according to his testimony, given electric shocks. For several days, he was denied food and water. He was brought to the limits of his resistance. This situation culminated one evening when, semiconscious, he swayed unsteadily toward one of the detectives, hoping that he would consider it an attack and shoot and kill him. The detective did not shoot. Both of them fell to the ground, and that's how other police officers found them and responded violently.

His wife, Alicia Herrera, a lawyer, who had been desperately searching for him, found out where he was. She had been forced out of her position as a judge, but she still had contact with people within the judiciary, and she also knew Cardinal Silva Henríquez. One of those high functionaries intervened during the night and released Jiliberto. After a lot of bureaucratic procedures, he was sent to Dawson. He arrived in January 1974.

After the coup, José Tohá's first instinct was to serve as a protector and inspiration to the rest of his colleagues. From the start, he took a

47. The DINA (National Intelligence Directorate) was formed in late 1973 at Pinochet's behest as a secret police. It was best described by a US military attaché as a "Chilean Gestapo," and it became notorious for its clandestine centers of interrogation, torture, and murder. The DINA was dissolved in 1977 but replaced by the very similar CNI (National Information Center).

dignified position, and he made a point of always trying to lift our spirits. He was on the front line protecting us from the violence and accusations against us.

José was deeply saddened by the death of his great friend Salvador Allende, with whom he had shared the struggle for common ideals. During the time that José was minister of defense, he also was friendly with many of the higher officers in the armed forces. Many of them came to his home and vice versa; he had cultivated relationships with many of them. When he left the Ministry of Defense shortly before the coup, he was decorated in a beautiful ceremony that the president attended. I remember how the president conveyed the admiration that many of the men in uniform felt toward Tohá.

So José—who was also very sensitive—experienced everything that we were living through even more intensely. In the first couple of months, he lost a dangerous amount of weight. According to a later account by Puccio's wife, when Tohá and Puccio were taken to the hospital in Punta Arenas in December, they had another shocking experience. They were brought to the hospital tied to the ship's mast, exposed to the freezing wind. Tohá was weak and fainted twice. At the hospital, they kept the lights on day and night and continuously changed the meal schedule so that they would lose all sense of time.

When their wives, Miriam and Moy, were authorized to enter the hospital and see them for the first time since September 11, soldiers were always in the rooms controlling the conversation. Many times when one of the wives would ask her husband a question or vice versa, the soldier would intervene, saying "objectionable question."

A few days after he was brought back to Dawson from Punta Arenas, José's health started to deteriorate again. We had shared the same room in Compingim and the same barracks at Río Chico. Often we would sit on his bunk at the foot of the bed, talking and listening to his animated stories. I clearly remember those last days in January before he was sent back to Santiago: lying in his bed very gaunt without an ounce of strength.

On the night before we were told that José was leaving, Commander Fellay came to the infirmary where we all were with José, and he closed the door and told him deferentially, "Sir, I've learned that you will be brought to Santiago and then to your home. You've been through so much ill fortune and so many problems, but very soon you'll be in better conditions. Don't worry about your brother Jaime; we have information that he will soon be sent to Santiago as well."

The ambience surrounding his departure, and the commander's words, made us believe that things would improve. I'll never forget the moment that Tohá left: as he left our barbed wire enclosure, he raised his arms and said:

"Chin up, we'll be okay soon." That was the last time we saw him. We didn't hear news of him from the day that he left—January 15—until his death.

One evening around seven thirty, some people were glued to the radio as usual. We were clustered in a little group, and for some reason I stood up and continued talking to the group over my shoulder as I walked toward the area where José had slept. Jaime was in the top bunk of the bed. Then I saw Andrés Sepúlveda coming toward me with his eyes wide, telling me to be quiet. I asked what had happened. "Something terrible: Jaime heard that José is dead." I ran toward Jaime and saw his radio thrown on the floor, he was covering his face and sobbing. Indeed, Jaime had just heard on the radio that José had committed suicide by hanging himself with a belt in the hospital, according to the official story.

It's hard to express what we felt collectively at that moment. We all cried silently. Jirón, with his characteristically gritty rationality, went over to Jaime and, to make sure that he wouldn't have a nervous breakdown, gave him a tranquilizer. The rest of us didn't know what to do through that sleepless night. We debated the painful conjectures about what had happened—none of us believed that it was suicide. But why had the situation come to this? What was his death worth? What had really happened?

Just a few days earlier when we were working, we heard on the radio that General Bachelet, Hugo Miranda's relative and good friend, had died. Just months earlier, Hugo had received a beautiful letter from Bachelet, which we all read as it made its way around the barracks. The letter described how much he had suffered and asked whether it was worth it to go on living in such a dehumanized world.

How was it that José's death caused no public reaction? How did these facts not weigh on the conscience of those involved? How could so many brutal acts of violence be carried out in Chile, a country where institutions, democracy, and moderation had always reigned? It was unbelievable to us that these values could be trampled on so easily.

Jaime responded to the tragic news with renewed resolve. His brother's death gave him a higher purpose: we needed to move forward, for our country and for ourselves.

The government was silent about José's death. We all thought that Jaime would be sent to Santiago to attend the funeral and to be with José's widow, children, and elderly mother. Nothing happened. On the contrary, a day or two later Jaime drafted telegrams for his mother and sister-in-law and her children, letting them know that he was okay and that José's life had a higher meaning and that his death would go down in history. The cables were prohibited from being sent.

After we left Dawson, we learned that José had been sent to the military hospital and then to the War Academy of the air force. The treatment that he received, coupled with his deteriorating physical state, had plunged him into depression.

Almeyda suffered similar treatments. After he left Dawson in January, he was brought to the Tacna Regiment. At first he was kept in isolation and prohibited from reading or receiving visitors. A few days later, thanks to his wife Irma's relentless efforts, his status was changed and they allowed his family to visit and improved his nutrition so that he would recover some of the ten to fifteen kilos that he had lost. He was permitted to read books and do some activities.

Suddenly, he was transferred without notice, and when his wife went to visit him he was no longer there. The same thing happened to José's wife, Moy, before José Tohá died. Irma started knocking on every door to find out where her husband was. Later she learned that he had been brought to the War Academy of the air force. When the prisoners were brought into that academy, they were blindfolded and all their belongings were confiscated. They wore blue overalls and were not permitted to communicate with the outside world. Almeyda spent several days blindfolded. Through this process, they were being "softened" to prepare them for the interrogations. Still blindfolded, they would be interrogated by a military prosecutor in sessions that were a mix of violence and transaction. They were cursed at, threatened, and subjected to an alternation of scare tactics and persuasive arguments, insinuating that if they were willing to sign a document, the interrogations would end.

Many of them were forced to sign documents blindfolded, especially people of limited means, with fewer defense mechanisms and less protection. When Clodomiro was subjected to this treatment, his health deteriorated rapidly—in those situations it was difficult to maintain psychological stability.

Almeyda spent about a month in the academy under these rough treatments. Irma's visits to multiple authorities were futile: many of them didn't know where he was or claimed that they didn't know, including generals in high command. Others promised that they would try to find out, but they didn't. The apparatus of repression seemed to be independent from the regular command of the armed forces.

Finally, after much insistence, they were able to have Almeyda transferred back to the Tacna Regiment. He was there from January to June, when we met again in Ritoque.

Osvaldo Puccio Sr. also traveled with Tohá and Almeyda and was supposed to stay in the military hospital until the month of June. He was in critical condition because of his heart ailment and was subjected to harsh interrogations, adding on to the worry about his son, who was still in captivity. Despite his physical condition and the amount of medication he needed on a daily basis, he was brought to the concentration camp at Ritoque in July, without having been granted medical release.

The same thing happened to Daniel Vergara: his hand worsened, and he also had progressive facial muscle paralysis. Despite this state of health, he was sent to Ritoque.

A few days after our late-January interrogations at Dawson ended, we lived through another depressing episode: the arrival of new prisoners to the island. It was the second time that a large number arrived. The first was in December: then one of the prisoners was the Socialist senator for Magallanes, Carlos González Jaksic, who, after being mistreated, was the subject of an unbelievably cruel act. To recall the Plan Z, they used a bladed weapon to carve a Z on his back, and he was brought to Dawson with the fresh wound not yet scarred.

A similar case was that of a person I knew who had been a senatorial candidate for the Christian Left party (Izquierda Cristiana) in March 1973, who before that was councilor for the Christian Democracy party (Democracia Cristiana). The day after the coup, he presented himself voluntarily and was brought to an interrogation where he came face-to-face with a militant from his former party, who was a member of the Servicio de Inteligencia Militar (SIM, or Military Intelligence Agency).

According to his account, the torture began with the traditional scheme: blows, isolation, death threats, electric shocks. His arm and two ribs were broken. He was subjected to two near strangulations: he was raised onto a chair with a rope around his neck and told: "This is as far as you go. Jump!" Twice he had already jumped but the rope was loose and he fell to the ground.

For this second arrival, we could make out the profile of a warship approaching the coast on one of those gray, cold, sad Dawson afternoons. Cranes unloaded containers of prisoners, surrounded by armed marines. They disembarked on the beach. They were the first prisoners condemned by military tribunals that we had seen, and we asked who they were. The majority of them would be in prison for many years, after being subjected to processes that did not comply with the most basic judicial norms. According to their accounts, they were not told what they were accused of, nor could they contact a lawyer. There was a simple formality: with twenty-four hours' notice they would receive a file with false accusations, usually founded in anonymous denunciations, or in confessions by people who had signed under duress or while blindfolded in torture sessions so they did not know what they were signing. And there they were, all together, condemned to seven, nine, or fifteen years of prison, and some to a life sentence.

They were put into an additional barracks that wasn't yet finished and that had been under construction until the day before they arrived. Their courtyard was totally surrounded with zinc plates so that no one could see them, as they were deemed "dangerous." There were iron bars on the few, tiny windows, and they were confined to this small enclosed place: a real jail.

Their food was brought to them by three soldiers who didn't enter the barracks. At the barbed wire entrance, one of the prisoners' delegates would go in and get the food, which consisted of two big pots: one with hot liquid and the other with beans. They used mugs that they put into the pots to scoop out their portions, and then they cleaned and returned everything to the soldiers.

We didn't know who or how many they were. At first we could hear them leave their barracks and run around the courtyard; they sounded happy, despite the circumstances. They had lived through horrible things. To look at the sky, feel the cool air, and be surrounded by *compañeros* was a big change that brought them some happiness.

After two or three weeks, they started to come out and do forced work. We could see each other, and we made signs at them. Whenever anyone recognized former ministers or former senators, or friends from Punta Arenas, party comrades, schoolmates or workmates, he would get excited. One of the men in the barracks next to ours was reunited with his brother.

There were twenty or thirty men between seventeen and twenty-five years old. Most were students and workers and some professionals and technicians who worked in the region, mainly in agriculture or at the State Oil Company (Empresa Nacional de Petróleo).

Some months later, when the true nature of the air force's "trials" became known, it was said that the process these young men went through would be revised and that there had definitely been errors. For the same baseless accusations that in Punta Arenas resulted in a sentence of ten years in prison, in Valdivia it was two; in Valparaíso, six months; and in the north, they were shot. This group stayed on the island after we left in May 1974, and we never heard from them again. Later, the concentration camp on Dawson Island was closed and the prisoners were distributed throughout three different jails in the area, and some were expelled from the country and sent into exile.

At the end of January, army captain Mario Zamora arrived at Dawson and stayed until April or May.

From the start, Zamora was determined to implement punishment. The first time some of us saw him we were in the infirmary, and he had his machine gun on his back and was surrounded by other soldiers. He went from bed to bed looking at each of us. He stopped in front of Puccio Jr., looked at him, and said, "Remember me?" Puccio answered, "No, I don't know who you are." Later he told us, "Of course I know who he is. When I was detained in Santiago, he kicked me in the ribs. Then he made me pull out my hair and eat it. How could I forget?"

Zamora didn't have much contact with us at first, except to establish his authority by punishing us. That's how Jiliberto once again was chastised. One afternoon on the way to the barracks from work, Jiliberto and his group passed a small squad of prisoners from Punta Arenas and they waved to each other. According to Zamora's version of the story, some of the men raised their arms with their hands closed in a fist, and this was grounds for punishment. He took Jiliberto and two others from the Punta Arenas group and locked them in a cell for two nights. These dungeon-like cells were one meter wide by three meters long, with no light and a cement floor. They had to sit or stand, because there was not enough space to lie down, and they wouldn't have been able to sleep on the cold, wet ground.

During Zamora's time at Dawson in January, another group of visiting journalists arrived, this time from the United States. The way that the officers on duty received them revealed their ignorance and poor judgment. For instance, during previous visits in November and December, the officers in charge made it clear that we were in a concentration camp: they would wear their machine guns prominently. Then they would round up the prisoners outside, have us line up in single file and sing the national anthem, and then have us raise or lower the flag. This is how they showed off that they had disciplined the political prisoners.

But the foreign journalists who came were shocked by the camp and the treatment of people who just months before had been ministers, senators, or congressmen. They took photos and film for television, and they conducted interviews. When the guards stepped away, we told them what we were living through and sometimes we even spoke in front of the military intelligence agents, who were surprised that we would speak so freely of the situation.

On this occasion, they interviewed Letelier, Corvalán, and me. Later we learned that the material, together with interviews with members of the junta, had been broadcast on TV in the United States and Europe. We ran a huge risk by making these declarations, either of prolonging our time in prison or of endangering our families. But I believe that experience proved the contrary, because many of the people who had been interviewed were freed earlier on, to avoid the international pressures that built up because of them.

After that experience, the military decided that no one—journalists or others—could come to the island. Any time that a journalist, the Red Cross, or a foreign political representative had come, they left with a depressing impression of Chile. Around that time, rumors started that people at Dawson would be brought to trial before the air force tribunals, which meant a life sentence or the death penalty. Our destinies were shrouded in doubt and we didn't know what was going on or how much longer we would be there: Would it be months? Would it be years? Would we be sentenced? Exiled? Would they send us somewhere in Chile? Would we be imprisoned? To motivate ourselves and avoid desperation, we would talk through each possibility. This is what we called *caldo de cabeza*, stirring the pot. Later when we read accounts of prisoners at other concentration camps around the world, we saw that this was a common practice.

Staying active was key to maintaining psychological equilibrium. We continued with our stone carving and classes. We picked up the language lessons we had started. Also, there was another group formed by Carlos Matus (an excellent carpenter), "Negro" Olivares, Pedro Felipe Ramírez, and Miguel Lawner (who led the group), which obtained permission to build a small addition to the barracks with some leftover materials and firewood.

Carefully choosing the best-shaped posts, they built a cozy corner of the barracks where we would spend several months. It was the only place except for the barracks itself where we could be if it was raining. We built some wooden benches, a few tables, and a fireplace. That's where we would relax when we could, reading or writing our letters on weekends. The little corner was called, like the nightspot, El Caiquén Dorado (The Golden Goose).

When we couldn't go out into the field, we would dedicate ourselves to other activities; at that time, our favorite was playing bridge. We would break into little groups and organize tournaments, especially on Saturday afternoons and Sundays. Dominoes also became an important game to us. The championships acquired a certain level of fame. The most dangerous players were the Radicals Hugo Miranda and Carlos Morales, Anselmo Sule, and Jorge Tapia. They competed against Ramírez and Corvalán, Fernando Flores, and Daniel Vergara. Each team had its own personality, and as the championship went on, they became more impassioned. We also played chess, especially in those increasingly rainy months.

On weekends, we would sometimes have potluck "feast days." We would gather whatever food had been sent to us: eggs, onions, some pieces of meat and extra bones that we got from the kitchen. Once all the ingredients were ready, Alejandro Jiliberto and Camilo Salvo and others would cook them over a small fire in a corner of the barracks. When it was ready, we would line up with our mugs to have a taste of this wonderful dish that was neither beans nor lentils.

When we had the energy to play soccer, we would organize a pickup game in the courtyard in the late afternoon. One day, Jaime Tohá, who was always in a good mood and with a quick sense of humor, had the idea to put boots in the latrines. The doors of these outhouses had a space under the door and another on top, so that if someone was sitting there, one could see his feet from outside. Jaime put his boots inside to look as if someone were sitting, and closed the doors. Those of us who were playing soccer saw him do it and kept an eye on it. Every once in a while someone would exit the barracks and go over to the latrine. The three pairs of boots indicated that all the outhouses were occupied, and they would have to go back inside. The funniest was Sergio Vuskovic. He saw they were occupied and went back to the barracks. Five minutes later, he came back. The boots were still there. Three minutes later, he tried again, starting to look nervous. Finally, he couldn't help himself and he started yelling about how it could possibly be taking them so long in there. From far away, we could see how he was shouting and gesturing at the out-houses. At that moment, Carlos Matus, who was with us and knew about the prank, ran toward the toilets, crossed in front of Vuskovic, and burst open the doors of one of the latrines that was supposedly occupied. We could see the back of Matus's head and his shoes facing inward while the boots were facing outward, which made it look like he was urinating on the other. Vuskovic's face expressed total confusion. Everyone else was stunned. Carlos came out, slamming the door behind him. Vuskovic understood that it was a joke and went sheepishly to the toilet. A minute later, Lucho Corvalán came over and waited on the side. After a while, he yelled out, "Pst, pst, who's in there?" When he didn't get a response, he threw some stones in. Since nobody protested, he realized it was a practical joke and went in.

After Captain Zamora's tenure, Captain Varas arrived, also from the army. He was a direct and affable man. The day after he arrived on Dawson, he sat down with us and spontaneously said, "Man, this is very impressive: it's exactly like the concentration camps I've seen in the movies." He was accompanied by an NCO who seemed to have a positive attitude as well. At nighttime before we would go to bed, he would come and tell us: "Gentlemen, hold on: one day more, one day less."

Usually when visitors came to the island, we would be locked in the barracks. If we were out in the field and they drove by us, we were told to hide behind the shrubs and bushes. But in February we received a visitor who paid attention. It was Colonel Espinoza, the commander in charge of political prisoners; his office, Cendet, worked out of the building that up until the coup had been the National Congress. We had heard that he would be visiting, and we had already discussed what we wanted to speak with him about. He also came with representatives from the three branches of the military. When we lined up, Hugo Miranda asked to speak. If they thought that they would find a submissive group, they were in for a surprise.

"Colonel, sir," said Hugo, "the first thing that I want to tell you is that we are representatives of the legitimately constituted government. We would like you to tell us when we will be freed. We have been made prisoners here with no charges presented to us and without knowing our status. This situation is completely unacceptable, and it is a violation of human rights and the rule of law. We want to be set free immediately. We also want to inform you that in this camp there are a series of irregularities: we are subjected to forced labor, insufficient nutrition, and censored correspondence."

The group looked uncomfortable. Espinoza turned red. He said aggressively: "In the first place, you all have brought this country to ruins. You have broken what Chile was, and you've replaced the forefathers of this country with a bunch of cartoon characters. Gentlemen, in this phase of our country's reconstruction, each of us has a task. Ours is to run the country. Professionals are charged with helping in the reconstruction. And you are charged with being in prison: this is your contribution to the national reconstruction."

He left and only spoke with those who had urgent family issues. He said he would check on some people's cases to see if any of us could leave, because we pointed out that winter was coming and that if we remained on the island, the situation could end badly. Certainly, this was before the death of José Tohá. The information that Espinoza gave us was that at that time, the possibility of transferring us to Santiago or at least improving our conditions was under discussion.

I believe that later, the deaths of Tohá and General Bachelet obliged him to reconsider this position. A group of high military officers or influential right-wing civilians must have insisted that the coming of winter could mean more casualties. Apparently, another more extremist group tried to block our departure and to prohibit foreign visitors to the island. This was confirmed by something that happened a few weeks after Espinoza left.

One day, we were locked in the mess hall. We heard people saying that some authorities were visiting the camp. We were isolated for the entire day. Finally, we were called one by one and brought to the barracks. The military intelligence service was conducting a search of our barracks. Each of us was registered and our things inspected. They went through our books and papers page by page. Then they asked each of us if we had carved stones or if we had utensils for stone carving. Of course we all did. They took the prettiest stones and told us to keep the rest. Then they took the little wires or nail files that we used for carving and an officer took note of each utensil and who used it. This search seemed routine to us.

Less than two weeks later, a high-ranking officer from Punta Arenas visited. At about two or three o'clock in the afternoon, we were told to line up outside in the courtyard. It was raining, windy, and cold. The officer stood in front of us in camouflage uniform with his machine gun and all his war implements and harangued us: "We have detected a serious problem. Weapons have been found among you, destined to be used in an escape attempt or to assassinate people within this camp. Given these facts, I have come to tell you that this is unacceptable. You have taken advantage of the positive attitude that your caretakers have shown toward you. Any privileges you used to have will be taken away. You will be subjected to special treatment and harder training."

At first we were bewildered, and then we felt angry to find ourselves once again confronting a campaign of lies and humiliation. What worried us most was the political purpose of this falsehood. Was the intention to kill some of us with the excuse that they had found weapons? Or was this story invented to influence national and international public opinion and justify any drastic measures that they decided to take against us? I remember the feeling of impotence that swept over us; in spite of everything, we had still harbored the hope that there would soon be a solution to all of this. This new incident only worsened our situation.

Right after the officer's speech, the lower-ranking officers and troops were given orders to be firm with us, and they brought us back to our barracks.

After these accusations, our delegate went over to Colonel Reyes from the SIM. He told Reyes that the allegations were unfounded, that no weapon had been found among us, and this could be proven by the documents filled out by the SIM officers on the previous visit. Our carving tools, which had been facilitated by the military, had been confiscated. He told him that we had not carried out the stone carving secretively; several officers had even suggested that we have a carving competition, so that we could distract ourselves from our circumstances.

It was obvious that this officer was complying with a specific function: to denounce something false and make it real, so that more drastic measures could be taken. He himself had seen the little utensils that were catalogued as "weapons." He could also see that the average age of the group was between forty-five and fifty years of age and that several prisoners were ill. He also knew the island and the security measures taken there. It was obvious that he knew that the accusations were absurd.

We heard that Pinochet himself told people that two bags of weapons had been found at Dawson. We were alarmed about the effect this could have on our families. It seemed implausible that anyone would believe this story: to think that with presumably two bags of weapons we could take on the army protecting this island cut off by air and sea, and stocked with cannon, machine guns, and technical weaponry, was complete nonsense.

In the interval between the "weapons discovery" and the toughening of the situation (between March 15 and 30), we received the pen-ultimate visitors to Dawson.

It was a group of people sent by Willy Brandt,[48] consisting of a German senator who had been minister of economic cooperation, another parlia-mentarian, and an official from the German embassy. When they arrived, they were impressed by the way the camp was set up. They met with the party representatives, mostly the Radicals who were members of the Socialist Inter-national. They could see that we were in a critical state, one that could be fatal for some. They told us that just days earlier they had been with our wives and that they knew very little about our situation. They asked us for informa-tion and said that they would do everything in their power to fight for our freedom.

The Germans kept their word. They were able to get some prisoners out, even if it took a long time.

When they returned to Santiago, they met with Pinochet, after having spoken with the ministers of external and internal relations, but were unable to receive a concrete answer about our future.

The denouncement of the "weapons discovery" took place after the Ger-mans' visit, so it's possible that the whole thing was only a maneuver to block our departure from the island and keep us hostage, as we were told on multiple occasions. We had been imprisoned for six months, and it's possible that some high-ranking officers felt that given the strong international pressure, it was time to release us and seek another solution.

Meanwhile, our forced labor began to revolve around the pro-vision of firewood. There was a consensus, among both soldiers and prisoners, that it was necessary to gather as much firewood as possible in case we weren't

48. Willy Brandt was a German statesman and politician who was leader of the Social Democratic Party of Germany (SPD) from 1964 to 1987 and served as chancellor of the Federal Republic of Germany from 1969 to 1974.

transferred elsewhere in the country. Snow would start to fall at the end of April or beginning of May, and after that we wouldn't be able to get more firewood.

There were some trees near our camp, and we went nearly every day to gather wood. The rains had started up again and sometimes we were completely soaked as we worked. We only had a few axes, so we would divide up the work and rotate. Some people gathered trunks and logs, and twice a day another squad would carry the trunks on their shoulders to the barracks, where a third squad would chop them into smaller pieces and stack them up.

Around that time, we requested materials to protect the barracks. The rainwater had started to seep into the place and there were leaks all over, even above the beds. Some would sleep in contorted positions to avoid getting wet. It was cold, and the planks of particleboard and zinc didn't offer any protection.

We desperately hoped we wouldn't spend the winter there. The pragmatists among us said that we should be prepared for the Antarctic winter; others were heartened by the conversations between the German officials and Generals Bonilla and Pinochet, indicating that we would be transferred to Santiago in March.

One March day, they came to get Hector Olivares and told him to gather his things. Minutes later and with no prior notice, he left. This made us happy because every time that someone left it was as if a piece of ourselves had achieved some freedom. Later we learned through a cable that Hector had been liberated.

On March 20 there was a changing of the guard, and thus began the most physically strenuous and violent period that we suffered through as a group during our time on Dawson.

One day around that time, from our barracks we sighted a warship approaching the camp. Then several smaller boats full of soldiers were dropped off. A battalion of marines arrived in the new guard, along with several sergeants and corporals and the troops, commanded by a first lieutenant and two sub-lieutenants.

This was a team especially selected and trained to affect us. One of the sub-lieutenants, named Jaime Weidenlaufer, treated us with a violence and hatred that we hadn't yet experienced. Another first lieutenant, Tapia, also arrived accompanied by a sergeant and a pair of implacable corporals—a special commando of the marines.

A few hours after they arrived, the regime changed abruptly. They screamed orders for us to come out to the courtyard. They lined us up and counted us, while repeating over and over, "What did you think would happen?! Who do you think you are? You're nothing!" The lieutenant made his first speech as we lined up there: "I've come to restore order here, because this has absolutely fallen apart. Remember that you are prisoners of war. The treatment you get here is going to change, and you're going to receive instructions right now and tomorrow and every day, so that you learn to behave and understand the work that you'll be subjected to. For now, your schedule has changed. At night, lights out earlier. I warn you that from now on nobody in this camp can circulate without authorization, and no one can move. If you move or walk around, you'll run the risk of being shot. If we have any suspicions about your actions, we will apply the law of flight. Every movement will be controlled. No one will walk around the camp."

Then he gave his orders: "About face! March to your room." He followed us to the barracks, came in, made each of us line up at his bunk, and yelled out the new procedure. Nobody could move when he was present. If he came in unannounced, the first person who saw him had to scream at the top of his lungs, "Attention!" and all activity and movement had to be suspended. Each person had to get in his place until given the order to continue at ease. He looked at all of us, lined up, and began his memorable sermon: "Remember that you are prisoners of war. Get used to it. Forget whatever you were and remember what you are. You are nothing. I will make you soldiers, no matter what it takes. You will be subjected to special treatment, and whoever doesn't follow orders will be left along the way. I can't stand you. Any conscript is worth a hundred of you: at least they have a steady, honest gaze. I look into your eyes and I see turbidity. From now on you'll know who we are."

Then he turned the lights off.

The next day, the new rules were established with total rigor: we were warned that we would be submitted to military discipline and that our life in the camp would now be run under those norms.

We were under the charge of a corporal armed with a submachine gun who started giving orders immediately: stand tall, left turn, right turn, forward march. When the lieutenant called you, you couldn't walk over; you had to get out of line, turn to the right, and run over. If you made a mistake, Lieutenant Weidenlaufer would make you come forward, get you on the floor, and say: "Give me ten push-ups, now." For the older people, this was exhausting. One time they made somebody do push-ups and on the eighth one he couldn't do any more. "I can't do it," he said with difficulty. He received an immediate retort: "I can't do it, what?"

"I can't do it, lieutenant."

"Not only can you, but you will continue to do them. Up until now you've done them in silence. Now you will do them again, saying, 'One, lieutenant, two, lieutenant, and so on.'"

This type of punishment became the norm. Any time one of us didn't react quickly or made a mistake carrying out orders, it would be followed with the "Give me ten" procedure. Weidenlaufer would walk among us looking at us contemptuously. Whenever he didn't like one of us or thought someone was taking too long to stand or stomp his heels, he would say, "You there, give me ten." He used the familiar form of "you." And before our last names, he always inserted the word "citizen."

From his first day, the corporal set a quick pace that exempted no one. After a few days, he relented and allowed the sick prisoners, including Zuljevic, who had acute sciatica, to stay in the barracks. For the rest of us, the rhythm was heavier than we had ever experienced. We all had to work at the fastest pace, like in an old movie. The lieutenant would appear at random and it was unacceptable for him to see anyone not moving quickly. If he did, he would yell, "Attention, line up." He would start to count: "One, two, three . . ." Each of us had to run from wherever we were working and line up before he got to the count of three. He would shout some more orders and the speed had to respond to the commander's plans: "We're going to remain here, and we have to step it up to prepare the camp for winter. Insulate all the pipes so they don't freeze. Reinforce the barracks to keep the cold out. Create a drainage system in the courtyard. Collect more firewood."

We would move large quantities of tree trunks to the courtyard and chop them up. Squads were established to carry the wood. The prison guards would keep watch so that all the trunks had more or less the same diameter and none of us were left behind. All this work had to be done at a jog, which was impossible when carrying heavy loads, so they established that we could walk if we were carrying things, and we had to jog after we had dropped it off.

This task was alternated with gathering materials to fill potholes and puddles and repairing roads and paths. We would go to the beach in squads and fill bags with wet pebbles and sand—the rain was incessant by then—and we would carry the bags on our shoulders, going back and forth in rotation. We were constantly filling, carrying, and emptying bags, and spreading the gravel with no rest, to the point where they would time us. During the first days, they had one of us calculate the exact time that each group took to go single file carrying the bags, bringing them back, emptying them, filling them again, and so on. We could hardly walk and several prisoners were in poor physical health, with soaked clothing and trying to keep pace with this endless cycle. After a few days at this pace, people started suffering physical pain. Many of us who wrote letters that first Saturday after the imposition of the new regime transmitted to our families and friends this feeling of depression despite our best efforts to shield them from it. The day after we wrote the letters, the first lieutenant, who read and revised every word, ordered us outside and told us: "I have read the letters to your wives and I have to say that I was surprised that you insinuate that the situation here is hard. By doing so, you are going to worry your families even more. I have also been in the south for a long time: I have been in these islands for six years. I know what loneliness is and I understand what you are feeling, but you cannot transmit these difficulties to your wives, because they have enough problems."

It surprised us to see him giving us reasonable advice. However, something about his apparent frankness made us suspicious. The next day, he himself gave orders that the forced labor should be intensified. There we were, carrying bags to fix the roads on a hillside, climbing up the incline with the bags, descending, and climbing up again, for the whole morning. The oldest prisoners were panting and stumbling.

They also imposed a system whereby all of us would line up outside to eat. The cold was unbearable and we had to hold one position without moving. When an officer showed up, our delegate had to inform him, "Lieutenant, we are X number of men, all fine, this person or that person is missing," and so on. When they gave the all clear for us to go eat, we had to all yell out in unison, put our hands to our chest, and jog to the mess hall. If they didn't like how we did it, we had to go back and repeat it until they were satisfied. When we entered, we would get our plates, serve ourselves, and eat in complete silence. Nobody could get up without authorization. When we were done, we had to jog back to the barracks.

A few days later, they forced us to sing. They gave us the lyrics that we would have to copy and learn by heart within a few hours, with brief breaks to rehearse together.

At night, we had to line up in the main courtyard, and after roll call, we would start the singing competition among the barracks. In the freezing air they would order, "Sing 'Tambores y clarines.'" And we would sing at the top of our voices:

> Drums and bugles
> force me to leave
> soon I will be separated
> from my beloved country.
> That's why I'll never love again in my life,

adieu my beloved homeland
I must depart.[49]

Often they criticized our group—the oldest one—comparing us with the youngest from Punta Arenas: "These people don't know how to sing, they have no energy, they don't have enough strength to even give it a good try. They are going to stay here and sing until they get it right." And we would keep singing for another half hour, another hour, until they were satisfied with the song. Meanwhile they would be watching us. If they saw that someone didn't know the words, or hesitated, or wasn't singing loudly enough, they would take him out of line and throw him on the floor to do push-ups, always yelling out, "One, my lieutenant, two, my lieutenant . . ." When the poor person finished the push-ups, he had to yell out, raise his hands, and jog back into formation.

When we got back to the barracks, they would turn the lights off very quickly. We had to remain in complete silence and stay alert, because the lieutenant might surprise us by coming in at any moment, and we would have to jump up in our pajamas or whatever state of dress we were in and stand up tall without moving a muscle. If anyone was out of line, he was made to jog outside or do push-ups.

These punishments were fairly common. I remember one that happened to Aníbal Palma. The lieutenant arrived at the barracks and someone shouted out: "Attention!" We all stood at our bunks. At the end of the barracks there was a tiny bathroom where we took a shower at night. Palma was showering and hadn't heard anything. He yelled out, "Give me more hot water!" The officer was furious. He reprimanded Aníbal, naked, who had no idea what was going on. The lieutenant gave him a minute to get dressed. Palma patted himself off, put some clothes on, and went outside. They made him jog around for a bit. Then they made him pick up two buckets of sand, one in each hand. He had to stand outside in the cold holding the buckets for fifteen, twenty minutes until finally his arms gave out and the buckets fell. They warned him that next time the punishment would be more severe and sent him back to the barracks. Meanwhile, we had been tensely waiting inside without knowing what was happening or who was next.

At the same time, they ended our improvised heating system.

49. "Tambores y clarines / me obligan a marchar / de mi amada patria / me voy a separar. / Por eso yo no quiero / amar más en la vida, / adiós patria querida / me voy a embarcar."

"Gentlemen, you cannot keep on wasting firewood at night. We will not permit this system of night watchmen that you have set up, with one person watching the stove. So you'll have to make do with the clothes that you have, and turn the stove off at night."

Together with the exhaustion of the days, the frigid nights were enough to scare sleep away.

Our stress level intensified daily, and no one was exempted, not even our only doctor, Arturo Jirón, who at this point was tending not only to about 150 prisoners but also to the soldiers, the marines, and their families in Puerto Harris. His comings and goings from the barracks to the infirmary were registered three or four times a day. Each morning, Jirón had to cross the path between the camp and the officers' and soldiers' homes, then come back for lunch and return in the afternoon. At each trajectory he was surrounded by soldiers and made to stand against the wall to be carefully searched.

We had to maintain extremely short hairstyles. They would check our hair daily when we were in line, and they were always sending someone to the barber, who would shave our heads like animals without the least consideration. Then, always in a jog, the newly shorn prisoner would return to the group. Obviously these short hairstyles made us even more vulnerable to the cold.

One afternoon, we were jogging to the mess hall when in the last row our *compañero* Tacchi fainted. He was taken back to the barracks. Jirón, once again with practically no resources, had to treat the asthma attack that prevented Tacchi from breathing.

On one of those days, a corporal went up to the lieutenant and said: "Lieutenant, there's a *huevá*[50] on the ground over in the courtyard."

"What do you mean *huevá*"?

"Over there, look."

"Go see what it is."

That "thing" was Carlos Jorquera, who was lying on the ground. Earlier he had gone out alone to cut down tree trunks, which he piled up in front of the barracks, and had fainted in the middle of the woods. It wasn't the first time that this happened to him, and he had become paler and paler due to his anemia. When we were in line taking turns with the trunks, he had started to dry-heave and then collapsed. Finally we convinced the officers to let him rest for a few days.

---

50. Colloquial Chilean language extensively uses words derived from *huevo* (egg). In this context, the word *huevá*—from *huevada*—suggests something irrelevant and despicable.

We dreaded emergency situations because we were always at the mercy of whatever plane might be able to land, weather permitting, to transfer the patient to Punta Arenas or, if the sea was relatively calm, for the arrival of a cargo boat that might take two or three days.

As I mentioned, obligatory exercise had been built into our already physically demanding days. At 6:30 a.m. at the sound of the bugle, we had less than four minutes to dress and run outside in the dark to the courtyard for exercise. Then we had a few minutes to wash, have breakfast, make our beds, and tidy up. Right after that, we were off to gather rocks or firewood or dig to install the drainage systems.

After they ended our night-stove system, they made us switch beds: "Now, gentlemen, no one shall stay in his old bunk. I am going to personally assign your bunks. You, here, you, over there . . ." They took blankets away from anyone who had more than three, and we had to make do with what we had.

One day, Lieutenant Weidenlaufer addressed us: "When it's raining heavily and we can't go out, we are going to have classes. Whoever is in charge of a particular topic will present the written program, specifying what he is going to present."

We started to prepare outlines: history, physics, electricity. We submitted the programs. He called those of us who had put them together and lined us up against the wall: "Look, I have been revising the syllabi and I want to know who you are and what skills qualify you to give these classes. Let's see," he called on Letelier, "what are your qualifications?"

"Sir," responded Letelier, "I've spent several years in the United States. I've given classes, I've worked in the Inter-American Development Bank—"

"Okay, fine," he interrupted. "Next, you, what are your qualifications?" And he continued like that.

Then we submitted a proposal to study economics and the history of Chile. We got this response: "Here no one teaches economics or any of those subjects, because everything has a subjective interpretation and you will teach the wrong one. Gentlemen, here we will not accept any kind of interpretation. You have no authority to teach the history of Chile. So, for the first academic semester, we are going to start with physics, electricity, and English. Everyone will have to choose among those subjects. In the next academic semester, which begins after the winter, you can study another language or another subject. Everything in its own time."

Fernando Flores put together the program for physics. He had several books about it and he taught basic classes about electricity and magnetism.

Then he moved on to quantum physics and particle physics. Weidenlaufer quizzed him about the meaning of this and that, until he realized that his two years at the Naval Academy hadn't prepared him enough to continue questioning Flores.

Weidenlaufer felt that he was the "dean" of the "University of Dawson," selecting the professors, checking what we knew, and prohibiting the social sciences and history.

ﾘ

The last visit we received happened around that time, and it was a representative from a conservative British newspaper. He was accompanied by Lucía Santa Cruz, the daughter of the former ambassador from Chile to Great Britain, who was serving as his translator. She knew Letelier and Matte and their families. It was a rainy day, and after passing through the wire fences, they came into the barracks and witnessed many sick prisoners lying in their bunks, with pallid faces and obviously malnourished. The rest of us were outside under the rain, working. Seeing the prisoners in these conditions had a big impact on both of them. She seemed emotional and at times couldn't translate what we were telling the journalist because her voice was breaking. Later, as they were leaving, she said: "I truly never believed that among Chileans it would come to this. I am shocked."

The attack simulations at the camp took on a particularly aggravating intensity. When the signal rang that there was to be a simulation of an attack, we were to return immediately to the barracks. If we were far from our barracks, we were to remain motionless. Any movement or confusion would be considered an attack on camp security and the culprit would be shot.

To clarify this, the captain in charge of the camp called us over and explained that there would be two different signals. He summoned the bugle player to demonstrate the two—one would indicate an attack simulation and the other would indicate a fire drill.

"In the case of a fire drill," he said, "come out of the barracks and line up outside. In the case of an attack simulation, nobody should leave the barracks— if we find anyone exiting, he will be shot."

We pointed out that it was difficult for us to distinguish between the two different calls, and we could make a mistake interpreting the bugle call. So then we agreed that in case of fire, they would not only play the trumpet but also sound the siren twice. Then we would exit the barracks and line up outside.

One night, we were chatting before going to bed when a single bugle call rang out. We looked at each other, asking, "What was that? Didn't they say that if it were a fire drill they would also sound the siren?" Right after that the siren rang out and we all agreed to go outside and line up. We hadn't finished lining up when there was an unusual shoot-out. Fortunately we hadn't yet opened the door. We were paralyzed inside and we said to each other: "Nobody move: this could be a trap." We threw ourselves on our mattresses without moving, listening to the deafening rounds of bullets and soldiers running around for more than half an hour. The soldiers shouted out, "They're coming from here, they're attacking on this side! No, the attack is coming from over there! Move!"

Then they would yell out instructions very quickly, as if they actually were fighting against invaders. After a while, when it was over, we were relieved that we hadn't gone out.

The next day, we told the officers that they hadn't respected the signals we had agreed on. They blew this off, saying, "Bah, it was probably a mistake." Knowing their organization, it was difficult to imagine that they could make this sort of mistake.

What brings men to resort to this kind of action? When we asked ourselves this—what motivations our fellow Chileans, civil and military, could possibly have in order to act as they had—we could only feel heartbroken. From the beginning, little by little we realized that at least two things were happening simultaneously.

First, a large part of this treatment had been ordered from above: it wasn't something that depended on the mood of the person in charge at a given moment, because similar acts happened at other concentration camps. Our captors had received detailed instructions regarding what procedures we should be subjected to. Second, what helped aggravate or soften the treatment depended on the personal attitudes of certain officers. Not all of them were very hostile, only some. There were those who tried to maintain a distance, as if marginalizing themselves, and in some cases, there were those who tried to maintain cordiality, despite the fact that it was practically impossible.

Nonetheless, some of them, like Weidenlaufer, demonstrated an attitude that was incomprehensible to us. Now it was possible that many immature young officers with no worldliness had been conditioned to believe that this was a war and that we were their enemies. And we can't forget their social origin: many of the boys who entered the naval academies were from the upper-middle class. So they may have been more hostile toward people who had attempted to bring about a process of social transformation that from their perspective led the lower classes to rise up and rebel.

This attitude was also reflected in the way they treated different political prisoners, depending on how they perceived their status. When they saw signs of a higher social status—in the way that the person dressed or spoke or from their academic background—they acted differently than when they dealt with workers or farmers. Then they would assume a tone of superiority, and they treated those prisoners badly.

These factors converged, generating a hostile reaction among the officers of the Chilean armed forces. This was reinforced by the phenomenon of imitation of the stricter ones. No one wanted to appear soft or be accused of deference to the "enemies" or of not following his superior's instructions. But not all of them acted in that way, as some maintained a more humane attitude and an ampler criterion. The traditional conduct prevailed in those who maintained the "*constitucionalista*" vision of former commanders in chief, Generals Schneider and Prats.

The troops' behavior is worth mentioning. In general, they didn't meddle. If there were ever an opportunity for them to approach us, they were always good to us. They came from a different social sector and they had a different attitude. They even said sometimes that they were being watched. They were afraid that the lower-ranking officers would bring a case against them, and so they sometimes pretended to treat us rigorously.

But the case of the midlevel officers was completely different: they were older people, career military men, who knew both the troops and the officers. They were less afraid of being accused or treated poorly or punished. Because of this confidence, they maintained a less conflictive relationship with us. When the higher officers weren't around, they tried to have some sort of familiarity with us and sometimes even offered words of encouragement.

This team stayed with us until the end of March. One day, they simply told us there would be a change and that they were leaving. We were surprised, especially because this meant interrupting our preparations for the fast-approaching winter. We had been working nonstop until 8:00 p.m. every day to insulate the roofs, patch the roads, chop firewood, and carry bags of sand and stones, rain or shine. We had been under constant threat: if we didn't finish the work in a certain time frame, there would be no food for anybody. We often said to each other: "Fine, we won't eat, but we can't work at this pace until we pass out."

At the same time, we were relieved. We thought that nothing could be worse than what we had lived through, and some people even imagined that we would be returned to Santiago.

The truth is that we had no idea that it could get worse.

In mid-April Captain Zamora returned to the camp. This time he was accompanied by NCOs from the air force, an institution that had begun trials against its own officers. Because of this, some of their men would do their best to appear especially tough. From the beginning of the military dictatorship, all branches of the armed forces had discharged or imprisoned anyone who had supported the Allende government, including their own military members.

Among the officers accompanying Zamora was a lieutenant named Valenzuela, with a very unstable temperament, which would become clear later. Zamora had learned all he could about the norms that had been established by the navy, and he tried to keep up the previous pace with an even heavier hand, although he didn't have the same administrative capacity as his predecessors.

His first command was to declare that everything would stay the same as it had been before. The forced labor was kept up at a similar pace, but compared to the previous group of personnel who had been focused on preparing the camp for winter, this new group seemed to only be concerned with physically wearing us out as much as possible. The work became concentrated on hauling around materials in wheelbarrows and on our shoulders, always while jogging in line. They divided us into small groups and sent us off to the beach to fill the bags with sand and carry them back on our shoulders without dallying for one second. When we were forced to jog, the soldiers would run next to us with their guns to hurry us up until finally we were so exhausted we complained, "We really can't go on." And some answered: "What do you want us to do? We're being watched and we'll be punished if you let up. We understand you, but we can't do anything about it."

If before we had sometimes found a moment to rest, now it was impossible. The rains had intensified and we had to work even if we were soaking wet down to our underwear. At the end of the day, we would take off our clothes and hang them inside the barracks as close to the stove as possible so that they would at least air out. The clothes almost never dried completely, and so we were constantly damp.

At the same time, they ramped up the punishments. A few days after their arrival, we were digging drains in the big courtyard to make a channel for the rainwater. We were surrounded by armed men watching our every move and yelling out if they saw anyone slowing down too much. It was then that something strange occurred. They came and took away Luis Vega and Jaime Concha. They missed lunch and they didn't come back for several hours. They were brought before the officers, who accused them of having been seen during the fieldwork plotting to lunge at two of the soldiers, disarm them, and take control of the camp. This was very serious, so they were brought to Zamora, who interrogated them separately so that they would confess who had been the one to come up with the idea. Both of them rejected the absurd charge: they had been focused on their work, and they had never spoken about any such idea.

They were thrown up against a wall with their bodies at an angle, supported by three fingers: the thumb, index finger, and the middle finger. They held them like this for an hour. They were beaten on their backs and legs with the butts of guns. Since they still would not confess to this accusation, they were brought again to interrogation and were finally released. They were terrified, and their state and the situation worried us all.

After that, they took even closer control of our work: a soldier and a sergeant were stationed next to the place where we hauled the material so that they could account for the number of shovelfuls we threw into each sack and then yell at us to fill it more. Because of the weight of the wet sand, jogging with that load on our shoulders was exhausting. I was in good physical shape, but I confess that I would close my eyes and pretend that my ability to withstand their orders was being tested, because if I turned it around and instead thought, "This is so unfair" or "Woe is me," my capacity to bear the work would diminish. So I had to give myself a challenge, something to overcome, in order to continue at their demanding pace. Other soldiers watched the amount of firewood we carried. If they thought that someone wasn't carrying a large enough tree trunk, the whole group had to turn around and carry more.

One lieutenant took a strong dislike to Luis Corvalán. He started to watch Luis directly so that if we tried to give him a lighter load because of his age and physical state, the soldier would wait for Corvalán to jog by and make him stop so that he could check his load. He would take Luis out of the line and insult him: "What are you thinking, idiot? You have to do a better job filling up the sack. Go back and shovel some more into the bag. Who do you think you are?" We had seen others treat Corvalán with the same tone; Tapia, one of the marines, had once singled out Corvalán and started insulting him:[51]

51. As head of the Chilean Communist Party, Luis Corvalán was a particular target of an explicitly anti-Communist coup and dictatorship.

"What kind of job do you have, idiot? You think you're the shit, loser?" Corvalán would calmly endure these situations.

There were stricter rules in the mess hall as well. We would jog over to the mess hall from the barracks. If anyone in line uttered a word, they would yell out: "No talking here!" We sat down like robots, in complete silence. Valenzuela always brought three armed soldiers to meals. He told us: "From now on, we'll shoot the first person who makes a suspicious movement." We ate our food as fast as we could, with knots in our throats and in our stomachs. Every meal became an agony. The guards paced around us, looking at each of us and aiming their guns at our heads.

When we finished with our soup, Hugo Miranda—our delegate—would stand up to ask permission to get some more. On the first day, we were sitting at a big table with two or three long benches, so that in order to get up, we had to lift one leg over the bench and then the other. Inevitably there was some "disorder": the benches moved, someone's hand moved a plate. This provoked an immediate reaction from one of the soldiers, who started to shout his head off: "What are you, a bunch of animals? You weren't taught how to eat? You don't have any manners?"

The prisoners at the next table over had it even worse: "You're a bunch of horses. You have no idea what you're doing, beasts. You don't even know how to eat." We were told to sit down and start over: to ask permission again. We all had to stand up straight. Then the officer in charge said: "When I give the order, everyone go to the table, take your plate, and when I say so, walk slowly over to the line, fill up your plate without talking, and without asking for more."

There was no longer any possibility of getting a second piece of bread. Sometimes, our hunger was overwhelming. They continued with the same rule that when an officer entered the barracks, we had to stop all activity and stand still. We were not allowed to move if any officer was walking around; if we did, they pointed their finger at us or yelled insults. They never loosened their grips on their weapons or on the grenades at their waists.

Speaking of grenades: an officer called Valenzuela came into the barracks one night. He stood in the middle of the aisle so that he could be seen from all angles. He took one of the grenades from his belt and asked the delegate: "Do you know what this is?" as he tossed the grenade into the air and caught it, then threw it again into the air. He had a feverish look behind his thick glasses. Miranda wisely said: "No, I don't know." "Oh, you don't know? These are grenades, and they could explode at any moment. Listen up: you are all in danger." He turned around and left.

A few days later, they came up with another disagreeable surprise. They started to distribute letters and packages at nighttime. At about one in the morning, while we were sleeping and the air was freezing, they would open the doors that had been bolted shut from the outside, and a group of soldiers would come in with lanterns to see our faces. Of course, we were frightened, since we had no idea what was going on with our families as our communication had been cut off. Since the time that we had been falsely accused of possessing weapons, we had been forbidden from receiving newspapers, and our mail had become infrequent and heavily censored. We were cut off and had no notion of what was happening in the world.

After they came in, once we were lined up they read out a list of names. We had no idea what to expect. Then they said: "Go retrieve your packages." So the people named had to dress quickly and jog out to get their packages. An hour later, the soldiers came back and repeated the drill. They even repeated the same names and told them that they had received another package. Captain Zamora himself distributed the packages, slowly and deliberately, until about two or three in the morning. The next day, he woke up late, while the rest of us were out doing our exercises by six thirty.

The exercise routine had changed as well. We no longer did the five- to ten-minute nighttime exercises that the previous group had put into place for each barracks to do separately. Now we were all taken out into the common courtyard that had turned into a giant puddle with all the rain. All two hundred prisoners ran in circles in the dark, in lines of two or three, covered in mud, around and around following the orders of a very aggressive lieutenant—the same one who had harassed Corvalán and who treated us like animals in the mess hall. He would stand in the middle of the courtyard shouting out instructions for us to go or to stop and do push-ups in the sludge. One day, our delegate got out of the line to tell the lieutenant that in our group there were older people and people with health problems, that exercising at this time of night and in the cold and rain was dangerous for them. "We don't have any other shoes. We don't have boots, lieutenant." "It doesn't matter," he said, "there are no exceptions."

One morning, Captain Zamora ordered that all jars of preserves be returned, because no prisoner could have food in his possession, except for a list of approved items: two packages of crackers, one or two cans of condensed milk, one can of instant coffee, and one can of powdered milk. These products were nothing compared to what our families sent each month, intended to last until the next package. We had two hours' time to hand everything over.

We decided to eat everything all at once instead of handing it over. I have never eaten so much jam in my life. We started the feast with Spam, a veritable delicacy. One person had several cans of it, and we opened them all. Then there were canned peaches cut into tiny pieces so that everyone could try them. We did the same thing with some chocolate bars. Our two-hour feast that Saturday morning was unforgettable.

They also took away our radios and then demanded that we hand over all books and magazines. They went through our beds and drawers to see if anyone had notebooks that we had written in. We had to put everything on a big table. Over the eight months that we had been imprisoned, each of us had collected about a dozen books. Some of them were textbooks and others were novels or complete works by famous authors. They were very valuable, less for their material worth than for the company that they had kept us. When the officer arrived and saw the huge pile—there were about thirty of us in our barracks, so probably no less than four hundred books—in different languages and subjects, he changed his tone and asked: "Who are the prisoners in this barracks?"

It was a comical situation, because while the delegate described our professions and job titles, the officer's face became progressively surprised as he found out who his prisoners really were.

"Wow," he exclaimed, "there are some very well-educated people here. No wonder there are so many books, but we're going to have to take them away." He called over a soldier and ordered him to bring bags to throw the books in. Lieutenant Valenzuela stayed inside the barracks with us, with the submachine gun and grenades that never left his person. It was about nine at night and we all stood immobile in front of our bunks. Before the soldiers took all the books out, he told them: "I'm going to stay in here with these people while you take away the books. I want to make something clear: if anything happens to me in your absence, if I'm attacked in this barracks and when you come back you see that I've been disarmed, shoot at me immediately and kill me. Then kill everyone else."

"Yes, sir, lieutenant, sir," the soldiers responded.

In those moments, we could only imagine what kind of mental imbalance motivated him and what new problem he could create for us. He could easily set off a series of violent actions. Our lives depended on these absurd details.

Each of us had his own way to disconnect from our circumstances. I remember that at the beginning I used a "countdown mechanism." I set Christmas as a goal. I started to count down how many days remained until then: sixty, fifty-nine, fifty-eight, and so forth, so on the most difficult days when it was hardest for me to bear, I would tell myself: "If I can get to day zero, I'm saved." Once I reached that goal, I changed the countdown to March 11. When that day came and went, I made day zero be September 11, 1974. We all hoped that there would be some news at the one-year mark, and we clung to that date so that we could bear our daily lives.

As our objective was survival, we tried not to listen to the attacks and lies that were so prevalent on the radio, on television, and in the press. Physical exercise was another mechanism, which I did often when we were not under so much pressure.

Conversation also became part of our survival exercises. Politics was always on our minds. At first we rarely discussed it because we knew that it would be painful to recall the recent past. But then we began to consider different theories. We tried to predict the future of the military junta, and I have to say that many of our predictions did not correspond to what actually happened later. In general, we were all wrong. What we were doing was projecting, one way or another, certain behaviors that seemed normal to us in a democratic society with constitutional norms, and this was the same logic that we had seen applied over a long period of history. But the behavior of this new group controlling our country—which had a war logic that was entirely different from what seemed natural to us—taught us that a political action undertaken in a dictatorship caused different political and social reactions. Sometimes we thought that a certain event would cause the government to act a particular way in order to diffuse pressure or resolve a problem. But they would react in a different way with attitudes that seemed aberrant to us. We believed that the terrible handling of the situation would bring about, over time, a marked deterioration because while they could probably depend on the might of their arms for a long time, they could not do so indefinitely.

Around that time, we undertook a critical retrospective analysis of our own government. We looked at those things that the Popular Unity had mishandled and the major errors of its leadership, including our lack of knowledge about the military situation. There was also a fairly tough critique of the extreme left and their tendency to insist on taking unviable roads. We also could not elude our own responsibility for the coup, because we had been ignorant about the mechanisms used by the US government. We hadn't known about the investigation by the Church Committee of the US Senate[52]

52. Senator Frank Church chaired the US Senate Intelligence Committee in 1975. Among its findings—which have been published by the US Congress—is the intervention of the CIA and the Nixon government to create the conditions for the overthrow of the Allende government.

into the CIA's participation in the coup. While we may have known that police reports about the CIA existed, or antecedents in the Ministry of Foreign Affairs, the Allende government was not in a position to detect and then fight a general CIA plan to overthrow it. Certainly, no one can deny that the United States opposed the revolutionary process of the Popular Unity. But there were diverse assessments regarding the intensity and mechanisms that Washington would employ during the Nixon administration.

Contrasting our past concerns with the current reality, we were shocked by the enormous change that had taken place in such a short time. Under the democratic process, we had used political or partisan considerations in order to evaluate a decision. But the Chile of now was living through torture, death, repression, humiliation, and hunger. This reality put into proportion the dramatic new dimension of politics. Our past divisions seemed so absurd.

The experience that we were living through awoke in us a more human awareness of public action, a greater sensitivity about the facts of the daily lives of every woman and man, over and above cold calculations, whether they were partisan or personal.

❧

In moments when you can feel death close by, you gain an appreciation for the greatness of simple things. The final balance revolves around the fundamental qualities of solidarity, commitment, honor, and integrity.

Under those circumstances, one asks oneself what has been one's contribution in this life. Ambitions and disputes for power and positions become irrelevant. What is fundamental is whether there has been a cause worth fighting for, and if one has fully committed himself to it. If he has shown affection and dedication to his family. If he has planted a seed that could germinate. Giving becomes the most important thing, far above whether or not one attained this or that position, or whether one had more or less power.

Comparing one man to the next, the most important thing is not his wealth, nor his political image, his education, or his power. What remains is whether that man created more strength rather than weakness, if he was generous or selfish.

When one returns to normal life, he immerses himself in daily routines once again and it's possible to forget what should be a priority: one's soul. In retrospect, it's easier to notice what one gives up when one doesn't live each moment with intensity and commitment, in good times and bad, maintaining a line, respecting certain principles. The pretense of a young professional in planning out his or her life and achievements has little meaning. Everything can change in one unexpected moment, at a vertiginous pace.

One reconsiders the relationship he has with his wife, his children, his parents, because in those moments he appreciates love more fully.

In terms of friendships, I was lucky to count on the affection and solidarity of many friends who supported me in the toughest moments. Any gesture under these circumstances is worth a thousand under normal conditions.

At the end of March or April, the officers made us put on a show. I was in charge of the prisoners from Punta Arenas. They put together an orchestra and there was a lot of singing and laughter. We gave one of the orchestras the nickname "Give Me Ten" as a satire of the push-ups punishment. We also came to know a prisoner who gave a great rendition of the songs of Víctor Jara. I'll never forget him singing "Alfonsina y el mar" or "Te recuerdo Amanda,"[53] forever linked in my memory to Dawson. This excellent singer formed a small band and gave guitar and music lessons. He helped us a lot around the time that we had to learn the military songs when we were admonished and punished if we were out of tune or rhythm.

During those weeks the prisoners also celebrated religious holidays; both Catholics and Protestants from Punta Arenas received permission to gather for several consecutive Sundays. They read passages from the Bible and discussed them, culling what they could from man's noble struggle for what is right.

In April I received a telegram from my wife in Santiago, saying: "Dad seems to be coming out of the worst danger." It was the first news that I had received that her father was ill, and he would pass away just a few weeks later. It was a horrible feeling to be stuck in a barracks, unable to communicate with the outside world, feeling not only one's own vulnerability but on top of that— and which is much worse—one's family's.

On May 7 we returned exhausted to our barracks. We were chatting for a moment while the water was running off the roof and streaming down the windows. Suddenly, someone said: "Quiet! Don't make noise, because Jirón is ill. His ulcer is bleeding."

53. Víctor Jara, a famous Chilean singer and theater director, was arrested, tortured, and shot a few days after the military coup. His songs became a symbol in the struggle for human rights.

Indeed, Arturo was very sick in his bunk. That day, the accumulated stress from recent months had come to a head. As our doctor, he labored day after day in a small room tending to prisoners and sick military personnel. He shared his "practice" with Luis Belmar, a dentist from Punta Arenas who was also a prisoner. Jirón had helped many prisoners who had been badly tortured before their arrival at Dawson, both physically and psychologically.

In Puerto Harris he also had to attend to the children of the military personnel. Although he was respected as a professional, two armed officers followed his every move while he examined patients. He bore this burden alone. At least the rest of us worked in teams and kept each other company. In contrast, Jirón began to internalize his daily struggle.

The hemorrhaging did not stop and we didn't know what to do. It was pouring rain: no airplane or boat would be able to get to the island, and Jirón urgently needed to be transferred to Punta Arenas for a blood transfusion. Some people kept watch over him through the night and we hoped that something could be done the next morning.

That day had been difficult: we had been working from nine in the morning until five in the afternoon in the rain. Almost all of us had wool or leather jackets, and our clothes were so wet that we were dripping. When we got back we had hung them on the bedposts to try to dry them out a bit. It was a dismal night. Many people knew that they wouldn't be able to withstand the situation much longer. I also felt that I was getting to the end of my rope, and although physically I was still able to bear it, I was desolate and felt my ability to tolerate the conditions wane.

We hadn't been able to rest at all when we were awoken at five in the morning. It was May 8, 1974. The officers under the command of Captain Zamora shouted at us: "Gentlemen, you have a half hour to gather your things, get dressed, and line up outside."

The scene plays vividly in my mind. We washed, dressed, packed our bags, and went out to the courtyard. It was dark and cold out. We all stood in a line, even Jirón. I spoke with an officer and explained Jirón's health situation, so that he would be allowed to sit. Once we were all lined up, they started to call us out in groups of two or three. We went into a room, they inspected everything, and they gave us back some things that had been taken from us when we arrived on the island: pencils, watches, radios. However, our identity documents were never returned to us. After checking us, they asked us—in a gentler tone now—to line up. We stood there outside under a freezing night sky in our still-damp clothes from the moment we were awoken until seven thirty. The rest of the prisoners—those from Punta Arenas and the condemned prisoners—were still in the barracks.

Little by little we started to have the feeling that we were being liberated from something big. It was a difficult sensation to define—like a step toward freedom, although we knew that none of us would actually be set free and that surely we would be transferred to another camp, but hopefully one where we could see our families.

After one final revision, we carried our bags to one of the dump trucks and set off on foot following the truck.

It was a marvelous feeling to leave Dawson. After so much rain, that day had dawned radiant. It was as if we were rediscovering the island. The sky, the sun, the sea, the steppes, and the trees shone in all their splendor. The landscape took on a new look for me. I'll always remember these images from our walk to the landing strip. The soldiers hurried us along, led by Captain Zamora, who had his gun at his back, hurrying us as much as possible.

We could perceive a heightened military presence. A torpedo boat was close to the coast, as if it were keeping watch over us as we marched. How strange to see a torpedo boat and so many soldiers guarding this group of thirty prisoners, on an island in the Straits of Magellan.

We walked a lot and came to an area that the rain from the previous days had flooded, taking down the small bridge. It would be impossible to cross. The truck drove through the river, and then Zamora told us: "You all cross any way you can." We crossed over the destroyed bridge, along some wooden beams, until we got to a sand bar. The freezing water streamed down at least three meters. A misstep would mean the risk of being dragged down by the current. We put down a plank of wood that swayed precariously as we crossed, clinging to branches.

Our bags and some sick prisoners were in the truck. We thought that the vehicle would drop them off and come back to get us, since the distance between the camp and the airstrip was about ten kilometers. But we kept on walking and we couldn't make out the truck in front of us.

We got to another, wider river, which was relatively shallow when the waters were low, which usually one could ford and cross without problems. But now the waters were high and the current was strong.

Zamora stopped in front of the river. We knew the area, so we suggested going down-river a bit so that we could cross at a narrower area. "Or we could wait and all cross in the truck," we said.

Smiling, Zamora ordered: "Gentlemen, straight ahead. We are crossing right here."

At first we didn't believe him. But he insisted. It was a disturbing situation: we had to get into the freezing water, running the risk that the current could carry us away. Zamora instructed the soldiers to cross first. They could barely remain standing. They went about five meters in and then they turned back. Zamora looked at us: "Your turn." We took off our clothes and carried them in bundles above our heads. As we got further into the water, we started to sense the depth. The water pulled us and froze us, making walking difficult. I wasn't sure if I would be able to touch the bottom the whole time and still keep balance. The current was powerful and if we fell we would be pulled several meters down. The water was so cold that it was like needles pricking our whole bodies.

We decided to make a human chain. Andrés Sepúlveda, who had a limp, couldn't hold himself up and the water started to drag him away. Several of us grabbed on to him to help him across. Finally we got to the other side; I dried myself with a handkerchief and a pair of underwear. Since I couldn't put the underwear back on, I put it in my jacket and put my pants on without underwear. On the other side, Zamora watched the spectacle. A bit later, the truck arrived, crossed the river, and picked him up to cross. The truck passed us and we continued walking. About five hundred meters ahead, Zamora stopped the vehicle and said: "Alright, whoever fits can come in." The eldest and the most exhausted climbed in and about ten of us continued walking behind the truck. Later Zamora stopped the truck again and said: "Alright, you guys can also get in."

When we got to the airstrip, we went down into a kind of sunken area. We were low to the ground, all in the middle clustered together without any room to move. In the highest part of the bunker, several armed soldiers were guarding us. We were there for close to an hour before we heard a loud noise. A plane, initiating landing, passed over us and took off again immediately. The turn-around might have been a security measure, in case we had taken over the runway. The plane circled and landed again. Two more planes landed. We were ordered to leave the bunker and march to a small building where the officers awaited.

A lieutenant, captain, colonel, and six or seven officers were in charge of the planes, as well as Zamora and the two lieutenants in charge of us: in total, a dozen men in uniform. Zamora lined us up and ordered us to sing. One, two, three different songs. Some of the officers looked away, perhaps disturbed, while others smiled. When we finished singing, they told us: "Sit on the floor." There, on the muddy ground, we waited until the engines started up. We carried our bags to the planes and got in. The planes took off to cross the channel.

When we got to Punta Arenas, we unloaded the cargo. The area was surrounded by people observing us and two soldiers on guard. We lined up and went with our bags to a place where we were searched again. They checked everything we had and confiscated any consumables. But the most surprising and the saddest thing was that they took away anything that would remind us of the island. They opened our bags and took out the carved stones and put them in a bag. "Gentlemen, these are the instructions that I have received. I must take the stones and make note of to whom they belong."

Perhaps they knew that the meaning of that symbol had already become widely recognized. Our wives had proudly shown off the stones that we had managed to send them. Many had them made into pendants. There was an artisan who said it was an honor for him to work with the stones and to attach chains for our wives at no cost. In seconds, the work of several months disappeared before us. It was pointless to insist that those stones were gifts for our families.

They also took the few things that had been returned to us from previous confiscations, even the ones that had been returned to us in Dawson right before we left: pens, watches, lighters. They even took a small jar from me, where I had collected some beautiful seashells for my children.

Then we were taken to a place that seemed to us to be so clean and tidy that it seemed almost shiny: it was the cadet classroom, and many cadets were walking around outside. We sat down to wait for some food. Then I saw something that shocked me. Next to the blackboard there was a large photo of La Moneda palace in flames and underneath a caption: "The fighter pilot does it best."

I thought how ironic and tragic it all was: that the bombing of the government palace and of the deceased president and commander in chief of the armed forces would be exhibited as an example of military success.

After we ate, some elegantly dressed men appeared and began to register us for the nth time, one by one, passing us through a metal detector. We had to remove our shoes and socks. They even ran their hands through some men's hair. We were dirty—that day we had woken early, marched several kilometers, crossed a river, waded through mud and rocks. The man who inspected me had a disgusted look on his face. Then we had to take our pants off. I wasn't wearing any underwear because I had put them in my pocket after using them to dry off after crossing the river. At that moment I realized that they had fallen out somewhere along the way. It was very uncomfortable to be naked in front of these officers. Then they took our belts and the shoelaces from our shoes. They ripped my jacket to take out the strings used for cinching the belt and the hood.

Then they lined us up in front of a large cargo plane. We boarded. The seats were lined up along the sides of the fuselage. Once we were seated, they tied our wrists together. Then they told us: "Keep your hands on your knees for the entire flight. Do not move them." There were three armed men with machine guns in the large plane.

We couldn't talk, we couldn't move, we couldn't stand.

The plane left Punta Arenas at about three o'clock in the afternoon. The trip to Santiago took four or five hours. We got to the capital at about eight o'clock at night.

As we disembarked, they removed our handcuffs one by one.

It was nighttime when we arrived, and we formed two lines. We were at the Los Cerrillos Airport, in one of the air force spaces. In front of us there was a group of people looking at us: some officers in uniform, others dressed in white (perhaps doctors)—and an important contingent of soldiers that we could hardly make out in the darkness, with their war uniforms, helmets, and guns.

Despite the scene before us and unaware of what awaited us, seeing so many people—some even taking photographs—was reassuring.

An officer came forward, Colonel Espinoza, head of the Office of Political Prisoners. He informed us that we had been transferred to Santiago and that he wanted to speak with each of us. He called me first. "Please kindly step this way," he told me. I got out of line and walked over to him, to an area illuminated by powerful light bulbs. They took a picture of me when I was in front of him, and then the questions began. Behind the colonel there were three people dressed in white. Espinoza asked, in a forced cordial tone: "How are you, Mr. Bitar? How was your arrival?"

For someone who had just left Dawson, it was a shocking question and it angered me.

"Fine," I answered tersely. All the situations and the memories that we had lived through were swirling around in my head.

"But, do you have any physical pain?"

"No."

"Are you physically well?"

"Yes."

"Good, we're glad, Mr. Bitar. Now kindly pass to the right."

I walked five or six steps and exited the lit-up area. Stepping into the darkness, someone approached me and said, "Over here." Then, two or three soldiers standing behind me ordered: "Get in the plane!"

Next to the plane that we had arrived in, there were two or three small planes. I got in one with room for very few passengers. When I boarded, a soldier with a very tense face pointed his gun at my nose. I climbed in carefully and sat down. I looked out the window and saw some fellow prisoners walking toward a similar plane.

I began to imagine where they might take me next. At Dawson we had heard rumors that we would be taken to a camp called Collihuay, near the Andes mountain range. As I looked out the window picturing this, a sergeant came on board and closed my window shade. Then, before the second prisoner came on board, he tied my feet and then my hands, and fastened my seat belt. He put gauze and plasticized fabric over my eyes. Finally, he covered my face with a cloth. I could sense that more prisoners were being loaded onto the plane, and then it was completely quiet.

Only a few minutes had passed when I heard a voice that said: "You have to take this man off to identify his suitcase." They took off my blindfolds and ropes. I got out of the plane and was able to say a few words to some prisoners who were getting in the plane next to mine.

"Where do you think they're taking us?"

"I don't know. I was put in a plane. You?"

"No. I think we're being taken to different places."

I found my bag, went in, and found three more people, from the group from Valparaíso. Then they tied and blindfolded me again. When the plane was full of prisoners—all blindfolded—two pilots came on board and the plane took off.

The flight probably lasted forty-five minutes. It was about 10:00 p.m. When we landed, they untied our hands and feet, but they kept us blindfolded. They took us off the plane, guided us down the small stairs.

Taking a few steps, I felt a wave of fresh air and I heard the sound of the sea.

Puchuncaví

Judging by the distance we had covered, I imagined that we were at the Quintero Air Base. My hands were handcuffed behind my back. Cuffed and blindfolded, I was put in a truck. There were mattresses on the floor. I was thrown onto them and I ended up on my back. Then they brought in other prisoners, squeezed us together, shut the doors, and started the truck. It was a closed vehicle and very little air circulated. Through the blindfolds we could make out interior lights and an armed man guarding us. He warned: "Don't move. Careful. Stay here. Stay there."

We drove for about forty-five minutes, thinking that we were headed to another concentration camp. The situation inside the truck was oppressive.

Then the truck stopped and they opened the door to let us out. Again I could smell fresh air. It smelled like stables. It was a cool night, but not at all like the nights at Dawson; here the air was warmer and sweeter. Two people took my arms and told me: "Don't worry." They led me forward. They removed our handcuffs and put us in line with the rest of our fellow prisoners.

Then a man came from behind and removed our blindfolds. There were nine of us, the seven from Valparaíso (Vuskovic, Vega, Tacchi, Zuljevic, Pinto, Marhoz, and Sepúlveda), Kirberg, and me.

Before us we could see wooden fences with barbed wire. Again barbed wire! Some lights came on and armed soldiers surrounded us. In front of us, a young naval lieutenant—about twenty-five years old—wearing a black beret introduced himself: "I am Lieutenant Labbé. You are in my custody as prisoners of war. You will live here at this camp. I want to warn you about a couple of things. First, in the event of an attack on the camp, all prisoners will be shot immediately and then we will proceed to defend the camp. Second, you cannot go near the barbed wire. There will be no noise at night. If we see any suspicious movement, we will treat it as a felony escape and shoot you in the back. Understood?"

Then he called us one by one and assigned rooms, all in a relatively polite manner. Besides the lieutenant there was an officer in charge of the camp administration, a navy commander, and a doctor who put us through a superficial checkup to report on our physical health. He asked us how we felt, physically, and if we were okay. Once again I had a curt response: "I don't have any problems."

"You don't need anything?"

"No, nothing."

Compared with Dawson, our room was luxurious. It had four beds and we were only two to a room, so we could put our belongings on the upper bunks. There was more space. The interior of the rooms was lined with wood and was more comfortable.

The next day, around seven thirty in the morning, we were called to line up. We had just come from an environment where we had grown accustomed to military instruction. At the designated hour, we jogged out and lined up. I was designated the group's delegate for our communications with the lieutenant.

I gave the orders to my fellow prisoners: "Attention, be still! Line up! Look ahead. Attention! Look to the left!" As the lieutenant approached, I ordered: "Look to the right. Look ahead. Good morning, lieutenant." His face betrayed his surprise at our military discipline and movements, which revealed his ignorance about our previous experience.

We realized that we were in one of the summer camps for workers, built during the Unidad Popular government. There were little wooden A-frame houses, built in a row, forming long pavilions. Each building had ten rooms, each with four beds. Outside the rooms there was a bathroom with nicer showers than at Dawson.

The temperature was a delight. We could walk outside without needing to jog or jump around. Nonetheless, it was cold at night because the windows didn't have panes—just a kind of wooden shutter—as they had been intended for summer use.

Suddenly I had the sensation that I had been there before. I could identify the place right away, because one of the chimneys from the nearby Ventanas refinery[54] was visible from the camp.

Additionally, the view of the town and houses indicated to me that we were at Puchuncaví, in a camp that was located just a few meters from a street. This was an enormous change for us, because we could see people passing by,

54. Ventanas is a smelting complex situated on the coast thirty-five kilometers north of Valparaíso.

children running. We could see houses and imagine that inside them, normal lives were being carried out. And to view normalcy, civilians passing by, a car, was very stimulating after nine months of complete isolation.

Later we learned that this concentration camp was named Melinka, and that the former prisoners used to sing an ironic song that was characteristic of the place:

> Here in Melinka
> everyone has fun
> the food is abundant
> for the sympathizers
> who have come to rest.[55]

There were other political prisoners at the camp, separated from us by fences and barbed wire.

Our pavilion had a small courtyard (about 250 square meters) where we carried out our activities. We could not leave that area and we were not allowed to have contact with the rest of the prisoners.

Regardless, strange things occurred. It had been a long time since Sergio Vuskovic had received news from his son. He knew that he was being held, but he didn't know where. During the second week at the camp, we heard some people talking in the courtyard adjacent to ours. Sergio recognized the voice of his eighteen-year-old son, Iván. Apparently the young man had been informed by an NCO that his father was also there, so he deliberately started to speak loudly near the fence. Sergio did the same and they recognized each other's voices.

As soon as he could, Sergio requested permission to see his son. During those days, Admiral Everhard, in charge of the Valparaiso region, visited. He knew Vuskovic from when he had been mayor of Valparaíso. At that time, they had seen each other and met frequently. The admiral had even been in Sergio's house several times. When we arrived at the camp, I, in my role as delegate, asked him a series of questions about our situation, namely when we would be freed. Everhard said that the prisoners from Punta Arenas would be brought to trial at the beginning of June.

Some people wanted to speak privately with the admiral. Vuskovic told him that the only thing he asked for was to see his son.

"We've received a request from your wife," Everhard responded, "asking

---

55. "Aquí en Melinka / todo el mundo se divierte / la comida es abundante / para los simpatizantes / que han venido a descansar."

that we allow your son to go to Yugoslavia, where he's secured a scholarship. We're considering it. Would you grant him permission?"

"Of course," said Vuskovic.

"Well, later we'll decide if he can go to Yugoslavia. For now I authorize you to see him."

That was an important day for us. Father and son reunited, and the boy was told that he would be sent to Valparaíso. When Iván saw his father, he hugged him and cried. Sergio tried to calm him down, but the boy said, "They're going to take me back to Valparaíso. I was there for a long time at the Silva Palma navy barracks,[56] where we were tortured. I'm so scared of going there again. I don't know if I'll be able to bear it a second time."

His father calmed him down and told him about the possibility of going to Yugoslavia: "Probably they're just sending you to Valparaíso to pick up your documentation."

Ivan was sent to Silva Palma again and spent a relatively long time there. Finally, he was granted a passport. While he was in jail, he got permission to marry; he was brought to his family home, where they had a party for him and his new wife. The whole time, he was surrounded by policemen. They let him be with his wife for a bit and then they returned him to prison. A few days later, he was brought to the airport, where he met up with his wife and they went abroad together. Once again I was surprised: an officer had expressed an opinion, and something different had happened, as if the repressive apparatus was working in parallel, not subordinated to the regular command of the armed forces.

We were treated much better at Puchuncaví than we had been previously. We were always under the charge of lieutenants from the navy, most of them from the same cohort as the first officer who had greeted us. Once he got to know us, he would come in and chat, because we were a small group of nine people and he didn't have much to do at the small camp except to come check on us once or twice daily. Little by little he stopped being "afraid" of us, and after a while he started sharing anecdotes. We invited him to have tea or a meal, and we fostered a more humane relationship that later extended to the other officers. At first they would come with a cold attitude, a bit fearful and tough, but little by little the situation improved. From the

56. The Admiral Silva Palma barracks were used by the navy as a prison and for interrogation and torture. They were under the control of Naval Intelligence from 1973 to 1976.

beginning, they showed concern about our health. Those in the worst health and the eldest were brought to the hospital for an examination.

Compared to Dawson, here we were contained in a smaller space, so the possibilities for physical labor were limited. When we first arrived, we worked on the terrain, cleaned up, dug trenches to gather rainwater, and erected posts to hang clothing. We got through that fairly quickly and then we requested and were granted permission to carry out other activities, such as language classes and discussions, which we did from May 9 until July 15, when we were transferred to a different concentration camp at Ritoque. Although we were stuck inside during that time, at least we were doing some intellectual work.

In general we would get up at seven thirty every day and be lined up and singing the national anthem by eight. We used one of the little rooms for our studies and the other as a dining room. Two soldiers would bring our meals to the gate at the entrance to the courtyard and we would go retrieve them. Generally our lunch consisted of a soup, another dish, and a piece of bread. Sometimes we received a piece of fruit for dessert. After we ate, we would return the rinsed plates. From nine to ten we would tidy up, and then we would start in on our activities. Some of us exercised every day for an hour. I continued studying German. Others studied Italian or English. At noon we had lunch. At twelve thirty we would return the washed pots. Then we would resume our work.

I continued studying cybernetics and economics. Around that time, we were permitted to have a notebook, and I started taking notes and analyzing the situation from 1970 to 1973. I recalled the facts and events and tried to understand the causes of what had happened to our country. I also gave classes in economics to some other prisoners. At around six in the evening, we were called on again to line up and sing the national anthem. We had dinner and at nine at night, we went into our rooms. Lights were turned out at eleven at the latest. We were allowed to have a radio, which was a big change for us. We were also allowed to hear some music, and we could get caught up on the news, which was so distorted and awful that to listen to it required a certain emotional discipline and resistance. But we felt a greater stability now that we were allowed to have books and radio and perform other activities.

When we arrived, the first thing we asked for was to see our wives and children, whom we had been apart from for eight months. This was granted.

I have such a clear memory of that Tuesday afternoon at about two o'clock when the lieutenant called for Kirberg and me and told us: "I have news for you. You are going to receive a visit: your wives are about to arrive."

It was such an intense emotion. Despite all the distance that we maintained with these officers, it was obvious that this young lieutenant was happy to give us this news, although he tried to mask it. "What time will they arrive?" we asked. "Immediately." And at that moment, I saw my family's car drive by on the path below.

We were euphoric. After having relived so many memories, having made so many plans for the future—if we were to have a future—what would this reunion be like?

We ran to shave and change our clothes. The lieutenant told us: "You stay here and I'll go talk to them. They just arrived and I need to give them some instructions before I let them in."

I waited in the room, looking out the door until I saw them arrive. They had to cross over some muddy grass to get to the barbed wire fence, open the gate, and come into our barracks.

It's difficult to reproduce the sensations I felt at that moment. I ran to my wife and it was impossible to contain my tears. We hugged and gazed at each other. There were so many questions about how the children were, our parents, friends. We didn't only communicate through words—more than anything it was just the feeling of being with each other face-to-face. She looked so beautiful. It was an injection of joy that helped us bear the situation for a bit longer.

After that first visit, we were told: "Now you have seen your wives. This will not be repeated." We insisted that it was necessary for us to see them, to be with our families. They relented and allowed us a second visit.

This time not only our wives came but also some family members. Parents, children, and some other relatives were permitted to visit. This visit also had a profound effect on me, because my three children—Javier, Rodrigo, and Patricia—and my parents and younger brother were also there. It brought me indescribable happiness.

Seeing my parents was marvelous, knowing that they had been very affected by this situation and they could now see me alive, although when they left they were rather anguished to the point where my father reduced his future visits to the minimum; he didn't want to see me behind the barbed wire, thin, with a soldier guarding us in the dim rooms, nor in this prison clothing. It was a mixed feeling—the euphoria of being together and the sadness of knowing that we would continue to be apart.

During the kids' first visit, I was surprised that Patricia, my youngest, had changed so much from the two-year-old I had left to the three-year-old she was now. When she first saw me, she was shy. She blushed and little by little loosened up and started to speak. At first she called me *tío* (uncle). I realized that during such an important time in her development, she had been fatherless.

Being able to see my family on a regular basis made me long to return to normal life, but this still seemed far off. Our wives would come, they would leave, they would return, and they would leave again. We would see our children for just a quick moment. The visits lasted forty-five minutes and there was no possibility of being alone with our wives. There was always an officer present, with the pretext that they had to be sure that we wouldn't "exchange information" or "discuss politics." It was very difficult for a husband and wife who haven't seen each other in eight months to have to speak loudly without a modicum of intimacy. Inevitably, we felt anguished.

When our families visited, however, they brought us food and clothing, which added another layer of satisfaction. We felt the pleasure of sleeping in a bed made with sheets. After the first visit, they brought us a big cup of tea and bread. We all got together and I shared my goods: we cut up the salami, opened two cans of preserves, and ate crackers. It was a pleasure to taste these things again. We started to put some weight back on and become more emotionally stable.

During the first visits, our wives updated us about our fellow prisoners from Dawson. We learned that they had been divided in groups of eight to nine people among the different branches of the armed forces and the police.

One group was in Las Melosas with the militarized police (Carabineros). Later they related that they had been kept isolated, forbidden from speaking except at mealtime. Others were at the Air Force War Academy. They were all crowded into one room and only allowed to exit into the courtyard on Sundays, *if* it wasn't raining. A fourth group was in the hands of the army, in very difficult conditions. They were isolated, incommunicado, and cold.

While we were at Puchuncaví, many of the men in uniform there expressed their concern about the lack of clarity regarding the political prisoners' situation. They often said things like "How is it possible that those prisoners have had these trials? How is it possible that the air force carried out such unfair trials?" "Such injustice cannot go on," they assured us. "Don't worry, a solution will come soon."

They were young men who tried to improve relations between guards and prisoners. Some of them even came back to visit after having completed their two-week rotation at Puchuncaví. One of them was really commendable: he had gone to the home of one of the prisoners in Valparaíso to ask his wife to send her husband a television set. One morning he arrived with the TV and said: "I'm bringing you this because today is the first day of the World Cup and now you'll be able to watch it."

Another officer—whose father had immigrated to Chile from Spain and who knew the sufferings of those defeated by Franco in the Spanish Civil

War—was surprised to now find himself on the side of the repressors. When he left the camp, he gave us his telephone number and address and asked for ours, saying: "I would like to see you again once you are released." And it came to pass: about ten days after I was released, this lieutenant arrived at my house with his wife in a regular car and dressed in civilian clothing. He inquired about how we were and whether we needed anything.

Besides Admiral Everhard, Colonel Espinoza also visited Puchuncaví, at the beginning of June. We reiterated that it was fundamental that we be told if there were any charges against us and when we would be liberated. Once again Espinoza said that some of us would pass through the normal channels of justice and others through the military courts. He added that the trials would begin in June.

A few weeks later, we heard on the radio that when the air force trials ended in July or August, the process against the "higher-ups" of the UP would begin. So we had a total uncertainty about what was coming, which only increased as we learned how ruthless the air force was being in the trials. We also heard that they were planning to involve some of the prisoners from Dawson, such as Clodomiro Almeyda, without having any formal charges against them.

Meanwhile, some newspapers published statements such as the following: "There are no more detainees, and the few that remain are criminals who will pay for their actions. They are imprisoned because they are delinquents. All trials have been carried out and the situation has been clarified for the majority of the detained."

Despite the fact that we weren't supposed to, at Puchuncaví we were able to learn about other political prisoners. At least once a week, a bus from the navy brought two or three prisoners in and took out another ten. When we arrived, there were about eighty detainees. During the first month, this number dwindled, and by the second month, we were the only ones left.

Some of them had been set free, and others were transferred to the Silva Palma barracks, where they were tortured again, and their situation remained unstable. Most of them were between eighteen and twenty-five years old. The fact that there were so few people left in the barracks filled us with optimism—we thought that our time in prison would soon come to an end. However, one night we awoke to the noisy sound of vehicles entering the camp. They were bringing another one hundred political prisoners from Chacabuco.[57]

57. Chacabuco was a concentration camp in the harsh northern desert of Chile built on the site of an abandoned nitrate-mining town.

Our illusions faded: Puchuncaví was being expanded into a full-blown camp for prisoners.

In addition to that disheartening realization, I also learned of the death of my father-in-law, Nazir Hirmas. When we were in Punta Arenas after leaving Dawson, I had received a letter from my wife telling me about the rapid deterioration in her father's health. He had had a serious heart attack and they had decided to operate on him and possibly send him to the United States.

On the morning of June 2, an officer summoned me and said: "Mr. Bitar, change your clothes because you're being picked up: your father-in-law has died. People are waiting for you outside."

I got dressed and went out. Four people from the armed forces or Investigaciones were waiting for me in a car. When I got in, they wanted to handcuff me. "Stop, it's not necessary, leave him alone," intervened one of the officers in front. When the car set off, they told me: "Yesterday afternoon we received the order to take you to Santiago so that you can view your father-in-law's body at church. Then you must come back."

It was a sad ride, full of mixed emotions, because although I was devastated, I was also being temporarily let out of prison and I would be able to see my family. Along the way, the people guarding me started asking questions to figure out who I was. One of them knew who I was because his brother-in-law had been my student at the Engineering School of the University of Chile and had spoken well of me as a professor. As it always happened in those cases, he justified my imprisonment by saying, "Some injustices are always committed." He agreed that everyone else should be detained, but in his mind my case in particular had been a simple mistake that should be corrected.

When we got to Santiago, they told me they had to go to the airport to receive my father-in-law's remains. "Your family doesn't know you're coming. We don't want any problems: don't move and don't distance yourself from us. If you don't want us to handcuff you, stay close to us."

When we got to the airport, they were told that the plane was delayed. So they decided to go downtown and they dropped me off for a while at a police station. They said to the officer on shift: "This person is detained, where can we leave him?" The officer put me in a dark room where they kept drunkards and delinquents, and they locked the door from the outside. I was standing and after a few minutes I could make out a motorbike leaned against the wall. The police officer came back and looked at me. "Careful with the motorbike," he warned. "If you scratch it or cause any damage, I will punish you."

A while later, one of the four men that had driven me from Puchuncaví came over and said, "Why don't you have lunch with us?" They brought us to a cafeteria, and after lunch we got into the car and went to the airport.

We drove right onto the runway. Kenny was waiting at the foot of the plane for her mother and siblings and her father's coffin. The people who brought me told her and a few others that I was there. Kenny hadn't known that they would bring me, and it was very surprising under the circumstances. It was a painful reunion.

My guardians had orders to bring me back to Puchuncaví straight from the airport. When they realized that I hadn't had a chance to see my mother-in-law or other in-laws and that the chapel wouldn't be ready for another hour, they told me, "Mr. Bitar, we're going to do you a favor: we'll bring you to your house, so that you can be with your children."

Meanwhile they radioed over to the other Investigaciones vehicle and a second patrol car was sent as back up. Now there were ten people guarding me so that I wouldn't escape or so that no one would try to "rescue" me. They brought me to my parents' house, where my children were. I hugged my mother and went up to my father's room, where he was in bed, affected by the death in the family. Immediately the guards came into his room to control our conversation.

My parents felt even worse seeing their son being guarded so closely. They invited the four functionaries to the living room and offered them coffee. The guards felt uncomfortable being treated so kindly.

I could only be there for a few minutes while I spoke with my mother-in-law and brother-in-law, who had come by to see me. Then they brought me to the church for a while. Later we returned to Puchuncaví, followed by the second patrol car.

"This must be very difficult for you," they commented during the ride. "What are you going to do in the future, when you're freed? What will be your attitude toward us if we see each other again?" Another question got my attention: "What would you do with us if you became minister again?"

One afternoon at the end of June, we were watching television and heard the announcement that Anselmo Sule—who had left Dawson with us and was in Las Melosas—had been set free unconditionally. This was an enormous surprise to us. The only explanation that we could come up with was that the meeting of the International Social Democrats would take place in the following days. Since Sule was president of the Radical Party—which belonged to the Socialist International—we supposed that the British, German, Swedish, and Dutch governments and other Socialist and labor parties in power in Europe at the time must have pressed for his release.

We also learned that Jaime Tohá, Arturo Jirón, and Carlos Jorquera were now under house arrest. This created high expectations for me, because it seemed to confirm the confidence our families had that soon there would be a resolution.

Among the many initiatives my father undertook to fight for my liberation was an interview with the minister of the interior, General Oscar Bonilla,[58] in January 1974. It was a curious conversation. Bonilla asked him how I was doing and what information he had about our condition. When my father told him about the conditions of my imprisonment at Dawson, Bonilla replied, "Yes. We, as military men, have the same kinds of problems. We are accustomed to living as if we were at war and eating nothing but beans: that is our way of life." At the end of the interview, when my father insisted that Bonilla explain the motives for our detention and how long it would last, Bonilla answered that we were "hostages."

Despite those responses, a while later my father requested another interview with General Bonilla. The general replied with a letter saying that he wouldn't be able to receive him but that he should be patient: things would be clarified and the trials would yield results. My father also went to speak with a Mr. Nocera, from the minister of the interior's cabinet. He said in effect that chances were good that I would get out: "Look, Mr. Bitar, here on this desk I have the papers for Jirón and your son. Both are awaiting the minister's signature. Both of them are decrees for house arrest."

I received this news two days before I saw on television that Arturo Jirón had been placed under house arrest. My heart jumped for a moment, and I thought that if the information that I had was correct, I might be next. Around then the air force (FACh) trials were ending and they had provoked a strong international reaction. This forced the government and the FACh, through General Berdichevsky, to declare that there would be no death penalty. From what we knew, the political effect of these trials was negative. That's why we thought they would not go down the same path with us. At the same time, however, we learned that a new concentration camp was being built in Ritoque, where we would be brought back together again to reduce the personnel cost involved in imprisoning us separately.

Meanwhile, daily life continued in Puchuncaví. Watching the World Cup provided a great relief for a few weeks. We also read. Around that

58. Oscar Bonilla was a leader of the September 11, 1973, coup and a political rival of General Pinochet with a populist touch. He died in a suspicious helicopter accident on March 3, 1975.

time, I got some magazines in German to continue practicing and the French newspaper *Le Monde* to read about the international situation. After a year of isolation, we had no idea what was going on in the world.

But it was not easy to receive these publications. Although my wife told me that they would be arriving, they didn't. I went to speak with the lieutenant, who told me: "Look, Mr. Bitar, the magazines are being delivered through the Naval Intelligence Agency, since we don't know German. You know that we can't have any information entering here that we don't understand. With regard to *Le Monde*, I've been looking through it and there's an article about Chile that is not written objectively. It's obvious that these French journalists are infiltrated with Marxist ideas. You cannot read that article."

Around that time, Ariel Tacchi was interrogated by two or three civilians who said they came from Cendet but who were actually from the Naval Intelligence Agency. Tacchi had been a Socialist councilman in Viña del Mar; unfortunately, one month before the coup, he had led the seizure of a settlement under construction, destined for the navy.

At the interrogation, he was treated harshly and angrily. Apparently they had come to supplement known information in order to justify his detention.

"Why are you being detained?" they asked him. To someone who had been imprisoned for nine months, the question seemed unbelievable and difficult to answer. Because he was a leftist, or because he was a Socialist, he said. But they weren't satisfied with these answers: "No: What did you do? What did you steal?" Tacchi tried to explain that he actually did not know why he was there. Their brutish response was "You're trying to tell me that you've been locked up for nine months and you don't know why?"

Despite the fact that the soldiers weren't allowed to come near us, they often had to come into our barracks to drop off our food. One morning, the guard who was supposed to be watching us with his gun from the other side of the barbed wire fence stood there watching while we ate breakfast. After a bit, he came up to the fence and said: "Look, I want you to know that I'm just a soldier. They put me in charge of this thing and I'm really upset that I have to watch over you. I'm not here to control you, but they forced me to do it. I've already been locked up myself several times for discipline. They've got us working hard here. I used to be a steelworker at the big Huachipato plant in the south and they brought me here, and I want you to know that I'm from the Popular Unity."

Having said that, he turned around and left. We never saw him again.

A chaplain also visited us at Puchuncaví. He was an older Spanish priest who was assigned to the navy. He seemed nervous and scared to come in. We received him cordially and he started to talk about human problems: the difficulties of those imprisoned and their families and the lack of food, money, and work. After a while, though, he affirmed that this imprisonment was necessary. This provoked a strong reaction in us. He said good-bye, that he would be back; but he never returned. I had asked him to bring us the latest declaration of Chile's Catholic bishops from Punta de Tralca, from mid-1974. He didn't send it. The impression that stuck with me is that some of these people were actually members of the armed forces dressed in cassocks rather than priests.

At 4:00 p.m. on Friday, July 15, an officer named Morera came over to us. He was always prowling around, and his job was to move prisoners. He was also responsible for transferring people by boat to Chacabuco, a former nitrate mine in the northern desert that the military had transformed into a giant concentration camp for political prisoners. In one of our conversations, he told us that while he was at university, he had also been a functionary of the Naval Intelligence Agency, and he had been in charge of surveillance of fellow students. Morera called us together and said: "You have half an hour. Get your things ready: you're going to be transferred."

"All together?"

"Yes, all together."

"Lieutenant, do we have to leave food items here or can we bring them with us?"

"Bring them—you might need them."

That led us to believe that we would be taken to another concentration camp. Since we had some containers that were already opened, we inquired: "Is it going to be a long trip? Should we leave open containers?"

"No, you can bring them. A special truck will be transporting you."

We packed our bags and left. When they opened the barbed wire gate, we saw the same gray truck that had brought us to this camp, with rear doors and benches along the sides. When we got in, they told us: "We're not going to tie you up, and we're not going to put armed men inside because we know you: we know that you'll behave. Don't worry."

We put our bags in first and then sat down and closed the doors. Inside it was totally dark except for two little windows high up, covered with iron bars. The ride along a dirt road took about a half hour.

Ritoque

They brought us to Ritoque, on the coast near Quintero, about two hundred meters of paved road inland from the shore and very close to the beach. Once again we were in little wooden houses constructed during the UP government as a seaside resort for the workers. But they had enclosed the area with high barbed wire fences and a wooden palisade on the outside.

Another barbed wire fence separated our barracks from the ones where the soldiers slept. When we arrived at Ritoque, the first thing we had to do was to "declare our assets." There were no other prisoners—we were the first to arrive. The navy personnel in charge of bringing us there handed us over to members of the air force. The commanding officer during our trip said: "I'm leaving these people to you. They were well-behaved." When we entered the barracks, they started going through our things. They went through every one of our books. We were allowed to keep our little radio.

From our rooms, we could see the summer homes on the hills, and we knew that from their balconies, they could see our camp and all of us prisoners.

The next afternoon, trucks began to arrive with other prisoners with whom we had left Dawson and some others who had left the island before us: Clodomiro Almeyda, Alfredo Joignant, Osvaldo Puccio, and Daniel Vergara. We hadn't seen Daniel for a long time, as he had been in several different hospitals.

We were very happy to see each other again, even under the circumstances. They told us of their hard journey to Ritoque. They had been in different places under the command of the FACh, the army, and the Carabineros. They had been rounded up in the morning, tied up or handcuffed, and brought to trucks guarded by soldiers in front and in back, escorted by other vehicles with armed personnel.

It had been a tense and tiring journey.

They were all inspected and assigned to other barracks. There were five pavilions, each with five rooms that could hold thirty-five prisoners. The barracks were in a horseshoe shape around a courtyard and a flagstaff. We sang the national anthem there twice a day. Watchtowers had been erected in the surrounding hills. Armed soldiers with dogs paced day and night, guarding us and also making sure that no one from outside would approach the camp. The circumference was lined with yellow spotlights that came on at night so the soldiers could perceive any movement. Still, for those who had been held incommunicado, in dark and subterranean rooms, Ritoque was a big improvement. Here we could talk to other prisoners, see the rays of the sun, and feel the nearby sea.

The camp was near a railroad line, and every morning at eight we would watch the train go by. Maybe the conductors knew we were there, because every day they saluted us with two whistles as they passed. The FACh was in charge of the administration of the camp, but all four branches of the Armed Forces rotated on guard, so that every fortnight a new team would take over. At night the Carabineros reinforcements would arrive. The armed policemen paced in front of the doors of our barracks with their dogs. They reiterated the instructions we had become accustomed to hearing: they had orders that in the event of any attempted escape or attack, they would shoot us all. Anyone who moved would be assumed to be an attacker and they would apply the "law of flight," which meant executing us by shooting us in the back.

A little more than a year earlier, workers and their families had come here to vacation during the summer. They had used these houses, and the initials and slogans of the different political parties were carved into the wood, along with *Viva Allende*, and so on. Even though the letters and symbols had been sanded down in an attempt to erase them, we could still make them out.

We were given some paraffin stoves for the cold. We would turn them on at six in the evening, and we would turn them off around midnight. That allowed us to heat up the freezing rooms and protect the elderly and the sick. Some of the prisoners had been brought straight from the hospital, like Vergara and Puccio.

Within a few days after we arrived, they had consolidated the thirty-five of us into one big barracks that had ten rooms with four bunks each. Then they erected a wire fence to separate us from the rest of the barracks, eliminating the courtyard where we had walked and confining us to a small area. They explained that in short order, some of the prisoners would be leaving and those who remained would have more space.

But things didn't happen like that. Around the end of September, another 150 prisoners were brought from Chacabuco. The camp became overcrowded.

The mess hall windows were covered over. Each barracks was isolated from the others. They began the attack simulations again. At around nine or ten at night, when we were already locked in our barracks, the violent shoot-outs would begin along with soldiers shouting, "Over here!" and "No, over there!" They would set off flares to light up the dunes around the camp. They always shot toward the ocean, as if our rescuers were coming from the sea.

◆

As in the other detention camps, the officers' attitudes varied. There were some who tried to distance themselves completely. There was one army captain whose name had been mentioned on Radio Moscú as a participant in violence or murder. He said hello and told us that he was in charge of the camp, and we didn't see him for a while. Later he tried to get to know us. He asked if we could get him a television for his room. In exchange he would let us watch TV until later at night.

Other officers—especially the youngest ones—had a more positive attitude. They acted as if they were just carrying out orders, and they tried to get along with us as well as possible. In contrast, a few were very awkward. One time, at about ten at night, an officer ordered that we all go inside the barracks. Some of us were late. He began shouting, and because he didn't know our names, he yelled: "Psst, you over there, psst, psst, get over here. Tomorrow you'll be punished: no going out for the whole day."

The next day, the punishment that awaited Joignant, Teplisky, and me was modified: instead of being confined inside, we would remove weeds from under the barracks. It was a light task and more agreeable than being stuck inside. An NCO on that team passed by the barracks later and, as he was closing them up, he said, "Look, don't worry, I am going to speak with my lieutenant. Don't pay him any mind. Hopefully tomorrow you'll be able to go out again." Once again we were able to appreciate a difference in attitudes.

When their rotation was up at Ritoque, these same NCOs said a heartfelt good-bye to us: "It was very nice to meet you. Good luck. This is all really very sad." We didn't experience any violent attitudes from them, neither at Puchuncaví nor at Ritoque.

At Ritoque, just as at Puchuncaví, the Red Cross came to visit the camp. Once again we indicated our necessities. We asked for paper and books, which were sent to us, along with a volleyball net and ball. We set up a small court and would play two or three times a day.

The Red Cross usually also gave us some information. This time they told us that they had spoken with Bonilla and Pinochet because at a certain point they had been forbidden from visiting concentration camps and prison cells. They had been able to reinstate the visits after warning the government that otherwise they would retaliate by making some of their confidential reports public. The Red Cross had prepared documents about the camps they visited, calling out the actual situation that they had observed. The reports were sent to the ministers of the interior and defense to ensure that the government was informed through more than one channel about what was really happening.

They told us that they were unclear about the government's position: they were receiving contradictory information. One minister would have one piece of intelligence and another would have a different piece. They had the impression that Bonilla was trying to clarify the matter.

We also received a visit—for the first time—from the Organization of American States (OAS) Human Rights Commission. Several older people made up the committee, and they were accompanied by a Mr. Bianchi, a Chilean who had previously spoken in favor of the government. We were doubtful about the influence that this commission would have. We were also fearful that any declarations that we made would be brought to the junta and used to keep us isolated from society and to delay our exit under the pretense that we would defame the government if we left the country.

Regardless, we gave them a general impression and we told them about how we had lived at Dawson. The members of the commission—a Uruguayan, an Argentine, a Mexican, a Bolivian, a Brazilian, and a North American— questioned us extensively and had lunch with us. As per usual in those occasions, the food was excellent, with two brimming courses.

As we were talking over lunch, the soldiers insisted that the commission needed to leave, but they took their time so that they could get more testimonials from us. At the end, a member of the commission told us: "In truth, what we've heard from you is nothing compared to what we have seen at other detention camps in Chile. We have to tell you that this is the worst thing that we have ever seen in our lives."

After they left, we didn't think that their visit would result in anything. We had been told that they would prepare a report that would be presented before the OAS General Assembly in about five months. So it was to our great surprise that one week after the visit, when they left the country, they put forth a preliminary declaration with a group of petitions to the government. Later, in February 1975, when I was in the United States, I read the Human Rights Commission report and it was frightening. It's one of the most important documents that commission has ever produced, precisely because of its origins: no one could say that this group was partisan of the Allende government.

The other visit was from a group of British parliamentarians from the Labor Party, who took a tour of the camp. One of them told me that he had a letter for me from the University of Sussex, offering a visiting professor position. He asked me if I was interested, because they were doing everything they could to get me out.

Visits from family members occurred on a weekly basis in the mess hall, from two to five in the afternoon on Saturday or Sunday. I was in the Saturday group. Around noon we would get ready with our best clothing. Each of us prepared the table where we would sit with our family. We would use a blanket as a tablecloth; we would set up a hot plate and a thermos, cookies, tea, coffee, and sugar.

When we had everything set up, we would stand outside, nervously waiting for it to be two o'clock. That's when the bus carrying our families from the Quintero Air Base would arrive. Our families would drive in their cars to the base and then would be searched before getting onto the bus. When the bus got to the camp, we would all pile up near the door watching them get off. The kids would come running and our wives and parents after them. Those two or three hours together were always very emotional.

When other *compañeros* arrived from Chacabuco, the number of prisoners increased and they began to schedule all the visits on the same day. It was a small place so we lost the sense of intimacy that we had had before. They also reinforced the soldiers guarding us and had the soldiers circulate around the tables with their machine guns throughout the visits.

They also traded their simple searches for more intensive ones.

Female guards were brought from Santiago and Valparaíso to pat down our wives. According to them, they had found out that our wives had been passing us written messages, which was absurd.

Fernando Flores's wife, Gloria, once requested that her visiting day be changed to an earlier date because it was their wedding anniversary. The guards made her completely undress and they went through each item of clothing and her hair.

Another change was the restriction of visitors to relatives only. Children, spouses, parents and siblings were allowed in. Our in-laws had also visited many of us. Pedro Felipe Ramírez's father-in-law, Radomiro Tomic,[59] came

59. Radomiro Tomic was a founder of Chile's Christian Democrats, leader of its left wing, and its presidential candidate versus Allende in 1970, when he ran on a platform closer to Allende's than to his rightist rival, Jorge Alessandri.

to visit him, and the visit was forbidden, despite the fact that he had requested permission from the Ministry of the Interior; the pretext was that he would have political conversations with detainees.

In the middle of the new crackdowns, there was one beautiful event: the baptism of Pedro Felipe's daughter, who was born in June 1974. The chaplain agreed to perform the ceremony on a Saturday, and anyone who usually received visitors on Sundays was permitted to attend as long as we stood to one side so that we would not communicate with the families of any of the other prisoners.

There was also a rumor going around that there were three different groups of political detainees: one group would be freed in Chile, another would be forced to leave the country, and a third group would remain imprisoned for a long while. With all these conjectures circulating, after our family visits we would gather outside to share information and speculate. These were the topics of our weekly conversations on Saturday and Sunday evenings.

Our wives suffered greatly from all this uncertainty. Forced to confront tremendous difficulties, they also had to continuously file paperwork to try to get their husbands released from prison. On top of that there was the economic cost of traveling to Ritoque each week. For several of them, filling the tank with gas for the trip, paying for lodging in Viña del Mar, and buying provisions was a financial burden that left them with a critical economic deficit.

Our activities at Ritoque began at eight thirty in the morning with the national anthem. Then we would have breakfast, consisting of a cup of tea and a piece of bread, along with anything else that our families had sent to us. Then we picked up our rooms and cleaned our clothing, followed by reading time. Generally around eleven, we would gather at the little volleyball court and some of us would play a pick-up game. Others would do some group exercise, and then we would have lunch. We took turns in teams of rotating "ranch hands," cleaning the tables and washing the dishes. Then we would go back to our rooms.

One of the most important activities that at least half of the group took part in was the study of languages and specific themes, such as reviewing the events of 1970–73. Some of us studied French, others English, German, and Italian.

Sergio Vuskovic was the "Italian teacher," and among his "students" were Palestro and Ariel Tacchi. I continued teaching French as I had done at

Dawson. By then my most tenacious student, Lucho Corvalán, had a good command of the language and was so obsessed with acquiring vocabulary that he walked around with a dictionary in his hand. The German group was made up of Clodomiro, José Cademártori, and me. Cademártori got hold of a record player with recorded German classes that we listened to attentively.

Fernando Flores organized a seminar that met three or four times a week in my room—about eleven or twelve of us—and we began working on the analysis of our Popular Unity government, 1970–73. I had been able to advance on this in Puchuncaví, and I presented my work to Almeyda and Matus. Later Letelier and Pinto also joined in.[60]

Miguel Lawner continued to sketch. He was able to capture the surrounding nature and portraits of us working, chopping firewood, erecting telephone posts, and talking.[61]

At the end of August, an event occurred that shook us up: the disappearance of Lawner's wife, Ana María Barrenechea, also an architect. She had been working to support the family and trying to get her husband freed.

On visiting day, Lawner received the message that Ana María had been detained by the DINA while she was working in her office. That Saturday only their children arrived, and they had no idea where their mother was. Some relatives went to speak with General Mendoza, but he, like other generals, was unable to get any information from the DINA.

After a week, Ana María was freed. We learned that she had been brought to an interrogation and torture center in Santiago. The questions she was asked were strange, and we never found out why she had been detained. We conjectured about the motive being Miguel's drawings. Perhaps they had been considered the basis for an "escape plan" while we were at Dawson, although he sketched in plain view of the guards. Miguel had handed over the illustrations to a colonel of the FACh himself, saying, "These are drawings that I've made. Could you please get them to my wife?" The officer responded: "Yes, of course. I will send them to Colonel Espinoza, who can send them to your wife." They never arrived.

60. Later, Bitar's analyses proved very useful in the publication of several books. Carlos Matus completed an internationally recognized report about new planning methods. Fernando Flores completed his doctorate in philosophy at Stanford University and then made important contributions to cybernetics in the United States. Clodomiro Almeyda continued to have an active intellectual production. Bitar continued to write what would later become a book interpreting the Allende period.

61. Later his sketches were published under the title *Venceremos!*

While we were at Ritoque, we went through a second round of interrogations, led by the same tax collector Jaime Figueroa. He came with three other colleagues. One of them interrogated me on the first day. I asked him if he had my declaration from when I had been interrogated at Dawson.

"No. They haven't given it to me," he said. "I've only been asked to come and ask you some questions. Tell me what percentage of these stocks you had in each activity with your father."

I answered him, saying that he could confirm the data himself because I couldn't remember the exact figures. Then he said: "Sir, there's something rather curious here: between 1970 and 1971, you didn't have a bank account. We've been going through your papers and haven't found one."

"Very simple. As you people know, I was not in Chile during those years. I was at Harvard University."

"Oh, okay."

Meanwhile they had also interrogated my wife about the same thing and they had asked her to hand over the deed to the house and the receipts for the cars. They had reviewed our bank accounts check by check and had consulted with my father at his office to see whether I had any interest or participation in his business. "Someone" had revealed that I sometimes went to an apartment in Viña del Mar—my father-in-law's—and the police had raided it.

Figueroa continued with the interrogation the following day. He was interested in copper: "I want to know about your responsibility in the handing over of information to the USSR about Chile's natural riches, particularly copper. You know that this could be simply a slip or it could be considered treason, and the consequences can be dire."

He caught me off guard and I wasn't sure whether to take it seriously or as a joke.

"I didn't give the USSR any information about copper," I answered.

"What do you mean? I have several files here."

"Indeed. Anything that you might have is recorded at the Ministry of Mining: that is the source for any information you are seeking."

"I have some of the files right here. First off, you were the minister of mining when two Soviet delegations visited the country, one led by the minister of industries and the other by the minister of geology, and you were the Chilean counterpart. What was discussed and what did you give to those people?"

"First, everything that was discussed is recorded in the Ministry of Mining. As minister, I was responsible for receiving them and putting together their visit. The schedule consisted of visits and sessions about machinery and technical assistance to carry out some production projects."

"You asked them for some things. What can you tell us about uranium?"

"About uranium, the counterpart was the Chilean Army, led by a Captain Soto, not me—you can verify that. He was acting on the orders of the president, who spoke with the commander in chief of the army. He was designated as the counterpart, and the whole schedule was carried out with army transportation and in places determined by the army itself."

"About copper, you gave them information about mining. This is a very serious matter."

I had to explain mining technology—extraction, leaching, grinding, and electrolysis—simple processes that the entire world knows about and that the Soviets dominated, as they were among the first or second producers of copper in the world. After I explained all this to Figueroa, he said: "Hmm, yes. What about the transfer of information about the reserves?" I told him that in Chile we knew little about our own copper reserves, because they were in the hands of foreign businesses. Chile didn't have enough equipment to do longer-term prospecting.

My interrogator took notes about these answers and emphasized that things weren't as they had been projected.

Afterward he interrogated Hernán Soto, Letelier, and Cantuarias about the same things. Around that time, they also carried out an extensive interrogation of Clodomiro Almeyda and Aníbal Palma, beginning with a series of tributary processes, especially against the legislators.

On September 11, 1974, Pinochet gave a speech where he announced that he would free the political prisoners, and he alluded to a possible prisoner exchange with Cuba and the Soviet Union. Later we learned that an earlier version of the speech had no mention of the Soviet Union nor of Cuba: the topic had been inserted at the last minute. The challenge to the USSR and to Cuba appeared as a precondition for liberating Chilean political prisoners. It was shocking to us that our release was being used as a negotiation tool with foreign governments.

Meanwhile, that morning was unforgettable at Ritoque. We had thought about commemorating the tragedy in some way or another, perhaps with a moment of silence. But later we reconsidered, because any action on our part could be interpreted as a provocation. It was best to go on with our daily activities and maintain the routine.

But at eight thirty in the morning, after weeding the pavilion, an FACh officer came to see us; he had been in charge of liaison with the head of the camp. The head was the commander of the air base of Quintero, with the last name Rubio; he had represented the FACh in Washington when Letelier was ambassador. Naturally they knew each other, but now he never appeared around the camp.

I knew the officer who was the intermediary between Rubio and us, because he had been the pilot who flew the president of the republic's helicopter, and I had traveled with him on a few occasions—to Rancagua during the strike at the El Teniente mine, and to Valparaíso. He often had lunch with President Allende.

That officer stopped in front of us and said: "I've come to speak with you on the occasion of celebrating one year of national liberation. We have liberated ourselves from Communism and Marxism, from a group of people who wanted to destroy our nation and who wanted to establish values, names, and people who were foreign to our national culture."

He continued: "Never again shall we allow Marxism to enter this country: we will defend what we have done with our lives. And now, the country will rise. We will also defend it with the lives of our children, because we do not want their minds to be corrupted. We know that in the near future many of you will be going abroad. However, we want to warn you that our intelligence agency will follow you to the end of the world. So be careful."

On September 10 Letelier had been let out, which made us very happy. We knew that Diego Arria, mayor of Caracas and a close friend of Orlando's, had recently arrived. The previous Sunday, Arria had spoken with Pinochet and the news was on the radio. On Monday afternoon, an officer approached and said: "Letelier and Puccio Jr., prepare your things: you will be transferred to Santiago."

Puccio's case had repeatedly been brought before the military authorities and even before Pinochet, pointing out that he was detained simply because he had been with his father at La Moneda on September 11. The answer had always been the same: "We don't know. People say that he has extremist tendencies, like the MIR." In August Puccio Jr. was interrogated. An officer from the FACh only spoke of generalities with him: What were his concerns? What did he want to study at university? How did he foresee the future of Chile? What were fundamental human values?

At around eight at night the truck arrived and they both left Ritoque. Days later we learned that they had been transferred to Tres Álamos, a concentration camp in the southern region of Santiago. They sedated Osvaldo, and at about six in the morning they brought him to the airport, handcuffed and surrounded by soldiers. People went in and stared at him, until finally the Romanian ambassador arrived, representing the country that had offered him asylum. They took his handcuffs off; he said good-bye to his family and boarded the plane.

Orlando Letelier was brought to the Venezuelan embassy, where he stayed from eleven at night until five in the morning. He went to the airport with the mayor of Caracas. Just like Puccio, armed soldiers escorted him, but when the Viasa airline pilot saw this, he said: "From now on, no one is coming on my plane with weapons." Once the liberated people had boarded, he announced on the speakerphone that he had the honor of flying with two people who had been detained on Dawson Island. One of them had been a minister under Allende. Several passengers applauded and toasted them.

Those days we had the intense sensation of being on the edge: would we remain imprisoned or would we be brought to trial? Or from one day to the next, would we board a plane en route to another country, where we would see normal people walking on the street, reading the newspaper, being with their families?

We had talked with Letelier before he left and agreed that it wouldn't be a good idea for him to make declarations right away, to avoid the notion that the former prisoners were leading a smear campaign abroad. When Orlando landed in Caracas, he said only: "It is like beginning to live again."

A few days later, when we entered the mess hall, we saw fragments of some newspaper articles with Letelier's statement posted on the walls. They were highlighted with red ink and they said: "Loyalty. Is this the loyalty that you have toward the military and toward Chile?"

The days went by, and on the afternoon of September 26 while I was washing dishes—it was my turn to be a "ranch hand"—a Carabinero came up to me and said, "Prepare yourself, you are going to Santiago." I asked him if I could bring my belongings.

"Don't bring anything, just move, because you're leaving and you're coming back tonight."

I went to my room and changed my clothes. I thought that I would be going to another interrogation. I remember that my wife had brought me a note from my lawyer about an accusation brought against Luis Figueroa[62] and me by the owner of a small shoe factory on Chiloé Street. She wanted to be compensated for some losses that she had sustained during the Allende government's intervention in the management of her factory. As ministers it was our role—at the

62. Luis Figueroa was president of the Central Unica de Trabajadores (CUT) and minister of labor. He died in exile in Sweden in September 1976.

request of the president—to sign a decree insisting on the requisition of a group of enterprises that would then become part of the public sector "social property area," over the objections of the Contraloría.[63]

My lawyer demonstrated that as minister of mining I had no relationship to shoe factories. I also didn't know this person or her factory. The handling of this situation depended on the minister of economy, industry, and trade. I had no idea. This had come about because, after the coup, the military government had called forward anyone who wanted to present complaints against the Unidad Popular "higher-ups."

I sought advice from the prisoners who were lawyers. They told me to take a blanket, because they doubted I would be returning to camp that night. "It's already getting late and they're not going to have time to bring you back, so take your blanket in case you have to sleep in the dungeon, which is always freezing." Just in case, I said to myself, I'm going to bring my notebook with my annotations about our analyses, which would later be published as a book.[64]

The transfer took place via ambulance, as they often did. Inside, three detectives told me: "We're going to Santiago. This is not an interrogation. There is an issue with a member of your family."

"What's going on?" I asked. "Is it my wife or one of my children? Is someone sick?"

"We don't know and we can't answer you."

I was worried, thinking that I was being released for another family emergency. Otherwise they wouldn't have taken me out of the camp.

They brought me straight to Santiago to the National Congress, where Colonel Espinoza was waiting. I went into his office.

"Mr. Bitar," he said, "you have been brought here because someone in your family is sick."

I asked if he could tell me who.

"I don't know, but it is an elderly person."

"Is it my mother?" I asked.

"I don't know, but it's an older person."

63. The Contraloría (Comptroller) is an independent government agency that rules on the constitutionality of government actions. During the 1970–73 Allende presidency, the Contraloría was controlled by his opponents.

64. Sergio Bitar, *Transición, socialismo y democracia: La experiencia chilena* (Mexico City: Siglo XXI, 1979). See also its English translation, *Chile: Experiment in Democracy* (Philadelphia: Institute for the Study of Human Issues, 1986), and Sergio Bitar, *El Gobierno de Allende*, 3rd ed. (Santiago: Pehuén Editores, 2013).

Alarmed, I called my mother's house right away. They explained that my grandmother was sick. The detectives said: "Okay, we are authorized to take you to the clinic, but first we are going to allow you to see your family."

Along the way I remembered that it was my daughter Patricia's fourth birthday. Later I found out that my family knew that I would be coming. My two older children knew about it but to Patricia they said only: "Today is your birthday and you're going to receive a gift. It's a gift that walks, talks, and gives lots of hugs and kisses." She sat waiting on the sidewalk in front of the house.

Along the way I asked my guardians to stop so that I could get her a gift. They agreed, and I was dropped off at my home in an ambulance with a box of chocolates.

My children were all sitting in front of the door, and they were surprised to see the ambulance until I came out. We hugged and kissed. I went inside. The policemen followed me.

"Sir," they said, "it's too late to go back to Ritoque today. We'll allow you to stay in your house tonight and tomorrow we'll go back."

My wife was excited and nervous.

"Your grandmother is very sick," she said. "She could die at any moment—she's in a coma. I spoke with Fernando Léniz and told him that there were rumors that you were going to leave the country or be under house arrest. I asked for his help to expedite your departure."

Fernando Léniz, who was minster of finance at the time and whom I knew well, had a laudable attitude, and he said that he would check. He spoke with the minister of the interior and said that indeed that had been the decision taken at the beginning of September but that Pinochet had backed out and that there was no chance of it happening. So Léniz called my wife and told her that he would do everything possible to get me out of the country within twenty-four hours, although he preferred that I would be free within Chile. He said he would try again for them to allow me to remain under house arrest. The minister of the interior's response was as follows: "According to this person's file, there are no specific charges against him. However, any favorable resolution has been delayed. I am not in a position to permit a favorable solution. There is a commission in charge of political prisoners. Despite all this, in the case of his sick mother [they thought that my mother was the one who was sick], I am going to authorize him to be brought to Santiago under house arrest."

Since my guards had said that they would bring me back to Ritoque, my wife began making phone calls. She called Fernando Léniz again. He called the minister of the interior to tell him that I was at home, so that they could put forth an immediate decree of house arrest. The procedure moved quickly. I asked the detectives to call Colonel Espinoza and his assistant, Carabinero officer Letelier, to inform them that the minister of the interior had said that the decree for my house arrest was in process. I heard them say: "Sergio Bitar is staying at his home. The minister of the interior has stated that the decree will be issued tomorrow morning."

"Fine, take him to the hospital and I will meet you there and give a definite answer."

At 7:00 p.m. I was taken to the Clínica Santa María to see my grandmother. The Carabinero officer arrived and told me that I had permission to stay in my house until the next day, when a decision would be made. "They will come pick you up tomorrow morning in order to appear in front of Colonel Espinoza at the Cendet at 9:00 a.m."

A policeman was stationed outside my house, and I was forbidden from being seen.

The next day, they brought me to the congress building, where I waited until noon, when Espinoza showed up. I was brought into his office and he was seated very formally with two officers on each side, and he said: "There are serious accusations against you. You are responsible for the nation's crisis and collapse and for the threat to Chile's unity. Therefore there are still important charges against you. However, for other reasons, after reviewing your file, the junta has resolved to allow you to remain under house arrest. This will be a temporary situation, for eight to ten days. Then a definitive decision will be taken. You can call for your things to be brought from Ritoque. You may not leave your house."

I began to lead a normal life. I spent time with my family and friends. A few days later, an order came from General Arellano Stark, from the Ministry of Defense, for me to appear at his office. When I got there an officer told me: "We have here an order according to which you are permitted to circulate within Santiago with prior permission from your local police station."

When I returned home, a police officer came to tell me: "The rules you are subjected to are the following: If you are going to leave your house, you must first come to the police station and communicate the place and telephone number where you will be and sign out. On your return you must do the same."

Things went on like this for a long time. At first I wasn't very worried because simply being in my house was so exceptional. I didn't think about the future: I was simply living in the present. Weeks went by, and friends came to visit more frequently.

One day Fernando Léniz came to see me, along with Jorge Cauas, the finance minister. I had known both of them for a long time and I had a good relationship with both. We had a very brief conversation. They asked me how I was. Cauas shyly extended his hand, and said, "Did they treat you badly? What really happened to you?"

Logically I wouldn't know where to begin to explain everything that we had been through in that year, but his seeming naïveté surprised me.

"The only thing that I would like to ask of you is to do whatever you can to get me permission to leave the country," I said. "I can't continue indefinitely under house arrest and it's clear that I can't stay in Chile. I have offers from US universities and from a British university."

"We'll take care of it," they responded.

During that conversation, Léniz said that he had previously made attempts to get me out, unsuccessfully. The more he had insisted, the more he seemed to provoke the military, and one of the officers told him, "You worry about the economy, and we'll worry about internal security."

A few days later, I received a call from the Ministry of the Interior: "In the coming days a decree will be signed ordering you to leave the country within a week, starting from the moment that the decree is communicated to you by the police. The minister would like to warn you, so that you can get your things in order."

I spent long days waiting. Some acquaintances came to the house and confessed that they had been afraid to come before. One time by coincidence four or five Christian Democrat friends had all come at the same time, and when they found that they had all arrived at once, they told me, "We're sorry but they could imagine that this is a political meeting," and they left immediately.

Walking on the street, I saw an unrecognizable country. People were quiet. There was little movement compared to before. I was surprised to see poverty juxtaposed with such a high number of latest-make automobiles. I didn't see many people I knew.

I received another phone call. General César Benavides, minister of the interior, wanted to speak with me. I went to the Diego Portales building and handed over my documents. The minister ushered me in a seemingly cordial manner.

"Sit down, Mr. Bitar. A decree will come out soon, mandating that you leave the country within a week. Why don't you read it?"

I was handed Decree No. 1749, from October 28, 1974, from the Ministry of the Interior, ordering me to leave the country within eight days, counting the day that I received the notification. If I didn't comply, I would be expelled from the country.

When I finished reading, Benavides added, "We know that you are going to a university. We have your information here and we want to give you a clear warning: do not make any declarations abroad. If you do, you will put your colleagues in danger. We can follow your footsteps."

So I answered, "Look, I have a contract for one year in an American university. I want to tell you that Chile is my country and that I love it just as we all do. No one has a monopoly on another man's homeland. I want to return to Chile. My question is, what will I need to do in order to come back?"

Benavides was surprised and asked his assistant, "What does he do to return?"

"Well, if you want to do so, you have to go to the consulate or the embassy and they will request your authorization. We will register all your information. We will be checking on all your activities abroad. And after we review it, we will make a decision. And now I want to tell you, Mr. Bitar, that even with all your good intentions, do not even think about coming back without consulting first."

Toward the end, Benavides added, "We know that you are a talented man and that you are going to Harvard University. I hope you give Chile a good name when you're abroad."

I remember so clearly the day of our departure. My family and I left our house to go to the airport early in the morning. I was searched from head to toe, as if I were a delinquent that people needed to fear. Many of my friends were still imprisoned. The president had been dead for over a year. It was such a different country, but at the same time it was my country.

It's Chile. It's the mountains, the sea, the sky. It's the people, their colors, their smell. It's one's own self. What a strong tension in my soul: being forced to leave my homeland meant cutting my roots. But at the same time, it meant recovering my freedom.

Boston, 1975
Santiago, 1987

Thirty Years Later

From the window I could make out the island, and then the runway. I had been a political prisoner there thirty years earlier. Now I was coming back, this time as minister of education.

The morning of November 21, 2003, was cloudy as the military plane approached Dawson. I felt my heart tighten, intuiting that I was about to bring closure to a long period of my life.

When we landed, Admiral Ojeda, commander of the Third Naval Zone, was waiting to receive me and one hundred other former political prisoners who were returning for the first time. I greeted him and stood next to him to welcome my *compañeros* from Santiago and Punta Arenas, who were arriving on successive flights.

Like everyone else, I felt unsettled. What would be left of the place where we suffered so much? I caught a glimpse of the landscape—cold, gray, and desolate—the wind, the twisted trees.

But it wasn't the same landscape. The navy officers were not the same ones. It wasn't the same country. We were not the same men.

Many of us were reunited on the island: Vladimir Arellano, Orlando Cantuarias, Patricio Guijón, Alejandro Jiliberto, Arturo Jirón, Alfredo Joignant, Carlos Jorquera, Miguel Lawner, Luis Matte, Hugo Miranda, Miguel Muñoz, Aníbal Palma, Camilo Salvo, Julio Stuardo, Jorge Tapia, and Sergio Vuskovic. Many others had passed away. Their children and grandchildren came,[65] as their lives had also been marked by what their fathers and grandfathers lived

---

65. In attendance were the children of José Tohá, Aniceto Rodríguez, Anselmo Sule, Julio and Tito Palestro, and Orlando Budnevich and the grandchildren of Osvaldo Puccio and Edgardo Enríquez, who observed with astonishment and emotion.

through. And there were many friends from Punta Arenas, such as Baldovino Gómez and Antonio and Carlos González, as well as Gastón Daroch, Aristóteles España, Américo Fontana, Rodolfo Mansilla, Francisco "Che" Marques, Carlos Parker, Libio Pérez, and Daniel Ruiz.

Clodomiro's widow, Irma, was there, and my wife, Kenny. She arrived on the last plane from Punta Arenas because there had been a free seat after all the former prisoners had boarded. She wanted to share this experience with me, after it had been so traumatic for both of us.

The officers brought us over to a large shed on the side of the landing strip, where they had prepared coffee, and waited on us in a friendly fashion. The tension lifted little by little. Slowly we began to talk among ourselves and share memories and anecdotes.

Father Cancino was there too. He came over to me and after greeting me affectionately, he teased, "Minister, you told me that when you were once again in the government you would make me Cardinal. . . . Here I am, ready when you are." I didn't remember that promise. We laughed. "Let's propose it, then," I told him.

It was he who, late at night toward the end of 1973, called my wife, Kenny, saying, "This is the chaplain at Dawson Island—" The connection cut out; Kenny felt her knees buckle as she feared the worst. "Don't worry, your husband's okay, he just wants you to send a German book." Admiral Ojeda told the other group that one day when he was a lieutenant he was sent to Dawson as an English translator for foreign observers who were visiting the island to check on our living conditions. "I thought that no one would be able to master that language," he said, "and I found Orlando Letelier, who spoke perfect English, as did other prisoners."

The moments we shared eased our spirits, and then we got on buses to go to Compingim, our first concentration camp. As the bus drove forward, I remembered the reverse trajectory, that May day in 1974 when we left the camp for the last time, on foot, on our way to be transferred to Santiago. I remembered the penetrating cold, crossing the river without pants or shoes, holding hands to stay upright.

When we arrived at Compingim, I didn't recognize it. Nothing remained whatsoever of the barracks where we had stayed. Our *compañeros* from Punta Arenas were the first to find the exact place; they took out signs from their bags, with the name of each barracks, and they planted them on the spots they remembered. Around each sign, groups of people began forming: Alfa, Bravo, Charlie, Isla. Some people took photos; others walked toward the beach alone to look for those black stones that we had carved so long ago. Many wandered around the field, following a trail of memories.

We shared a moment of silence, and we formed a circle to solemnize this transcendent moment. Several people spoke. There were emotional statements, poems, memories of those who were no longer with us, and a rejection of the dictatorship, injustice, and violence.

The men in uniform kept a respectful distance. Rodolfo Mansilla, sculptor and stone-carver, approached Carolina Tohá and said: "The day that your father was taken from Dawson, I was returning from forced labor. We crossed paths at the gate of the camp. As José was leaving, surrounded by soldiers, he stopped and took off his gloves. He gave them to me and said, 'They have protected my hands from this cold; I will leave them with you so they protect yours, too.'"

Mansilla went on: "I have kept these gloves for thirty years because of the profound significance that he and his gesture meant to me. Here they are." He reached into his parka and took the gloves out and put them in Carolina's hands. She paled, and tears ran down our faces.

We moved on and continued to Río Chico and then Puerto Harris. I couldn't make out the paths we had had to walk to circumvent the houses and avoid being seen by people in the village. We arrived at the church. It was smaller than I remembered, with dark wood and white banisters.

We climbed the stone staircase and then over the wooden threshold. We remembered the corners that we had each painted, under the architect Miguel Lawner's watchful eye, to assure that we would do a good job.

The officers and sailors had organized an ecumenical service. Father Cancino spoke, and then an evangelical pastor and a Masonic representative. Outside, Lawner read the list of those who were no longer with us, his voice cracking. We sang the national anthem.

Before leaving, I asked them to wait for me, and I went to the school in Puerto Harris. I said hello to the teachers and looked over the facilities. They told me that they needed a bigger space and more protection from the cold, and I promised to have it done. Inside I thought: what better place to instill education than on that island where we had suffered so much. Five years later, in June 2008, when I was minister of public works, I received an invitation to inaugurate the new facilities. And I was delighted to learn that the school director had recognized this promise kept.

On the bus going back to the base, I got lost in thoughts about life and its mysteries. I reflected about what had happened to me the day before the return to Dawson. On November 20, 2003, there was a celebration for the fiftieth anniversary of the founding of Puerto Williams, the world's southern-most town. The minister of defense, Michelle Bachelet, who had collaborated to facilitate our return to Dawson and who was supposed to accompany us, suffered an injury and was unable to travel. So I was tasked with presiding over the commemorative acts organized by the navy, in the presence of the commander in chief, Admiral Vergara.

Destiny has so many surprises in store for us! Thirty years earlier, in 1973, I was a political prisoner with no rights. On this day in 2003 I received military honors. In my lifetime I had the opportunity to rise from the ashes and contribute to rebuilding democracy in my country.

I remembered how difficult it had been for Chileans to come together and how difficult it had been to organize this very trip, thirty years later. Many people did not want to return to the island ever again, and especially not in the presence of the navy personnel, which could limit the spontaneity and personal expression of what was in their hearts. I could sense that the navy personnel were also fearful of reliving the past and exposing themselves to rejection.

To facilitate things, the night before the trip to Dawson, I attended two dinners in Punta Arenas. I had accepted an invitation to the house of the commander of the Third Naval Zone. General Arancibia Clavel, commander of the local army division, was also there, along with Punta Arenas's mayor Morano and the undersecretary of the navy, Carlos Mackenney. The gathering helped dissipate any anxieties. Then I went to a restaurant in Punta Arenas where a group of animated former prisoners were reviewing their symbolic activities for the next day's long-awaited return to the island.

In the midst of these thoughts, while looking out the bus window, I watched the afternoon fade. The intense hours we had shared had changed my mood. I felt calmer, more peaceful, as if a period of my life had closed, helping to heal the wound in my soul.

We got out of the vehicle and gathered at the airstrip to begin our return. The ambiance was charged with emotion. Admiral Ojeda said these unexpected parting words: "We hope that your stay was pleasant despite the pain. . . . We have done everything possible to welcome you here—with love."

There was a spontaneous round of applause that went on and on. The admiral backed up, bewildered. Something had shifted inside all of us.

On the way back to Punta Arenas, I was filled with the same sensation that had rooted itself in me years ago: indignation in the face of unnecessary suffering.

In 1984, just after returning from exile, I had gone to visit the concentration camp at Puchuncaví, where I had been prisoner in 1974, after Dawson. I walked up a hill to get to the barracks. They were abandoned—not a soul in sight. One of the doors moved in the wind and made a creaking noise that I can still hear in my memory, like a lament that only I could hear.

At Dawson there were no material vestiges; everything had disappeared. There was no trace of the buildings or the electrical posts that had been so difficult for us to erect or the wire fences that contained us.

The pain was in our souls.

The planes took off. But this time I didn't have to leave Chile to regain my freedom: I was free in my homeland and in democracy.

S. B.

Santiago de Chile
March 2009

Index

Page numbers in italics refer to illustrations.

Critical Human Rights

Printed in the United States
By Bookmasters